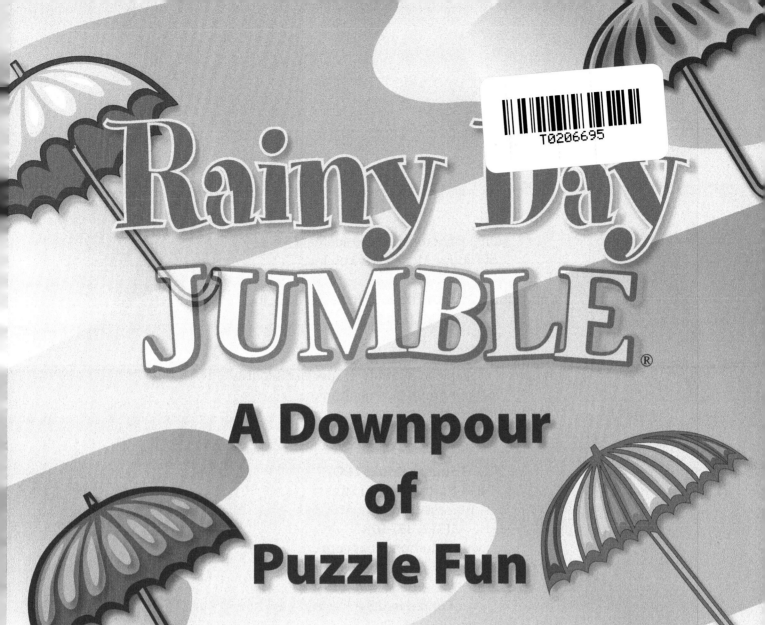

Rainy Day JUMBLE®

A Downpour
of
Puzzle Fun

Henri Arnold, Bob Lee, and Mike Argirion

TRIUMPH
BOOKS

This book is available in quantity at special discounts
for your group or organization.

For further information, contact:

Triumph Books LLC
814 North Franklin Street
Chicago, Illinois 60610
(312) 337-0747
www.triumphbooks.com

Printed in U.S.A.

ISBN: 978-1-60078-352-4

Design by Sue Knopf

CONTENTS

Rainy Day JUMBLE®

Classic Puzzles

JUMBLE®

Unscramble these four Jumbles, one letter to each square, to form four ordinary words.

WONNK

TOGAL

RUQUOM

GRATTE

Nice job! I'm proud of you

WHAT DAD SAID WHEN JUNIOR CLEANED THE FIREPLACE.

Now arrange the circled letters to form the surprise answer, as suggested by the above cartoon.

Print answer here "☐☐☐☐☐ ☐☐☐☐"

JUMBLE®

Unscramble these four Jumbles, one letter to each square, to form four ordinary words.

TUBOD

CITHY

TRYAEB

DEPIMN

I just had my nails done

A PAIR OF GLOVES CAN DO THIS FOR A GARDENER.

Now arrange the circled letters to form the surprise answer, as suggested by the above cartoon.

Print answer here ◯◯◯◯ IN "◯◯◯◯◯"

JUMBLE

Unscramble these four Jumbles, one letter
to each square, to form four ordinary words.

TYKIT

GNUST

SHAVIN

HINEAL

But, dear, I've been
so busy I didn't
have time

WHAT CHRISTMAS
TURNED INTO WHEN
SHE DIDN'T GET
A PRESENT.

Now arrange the circled letters to form the
surprise answer, as suggested by the above
cartoon.

*Print
answer
here*

JUMBLE®

Unscramble these four Jumbles, one letter to each square, to form four ordinary words.

MYKOS

LAPID

AMMBLE

HADILA

Gimme the ball-- You're all mixed up

Take second

NO!!

WHAT HE DID WHEN HIS MANAGER "TALKED."

Now arrange the circled letters to form the surprise answer, as suggested by the above cartoon.

Print answer here

HE " "

JUMBLE®

Unscramble these four Jumbles, one letter to each square, to form four ordinary words.

DESET

HILEW

MAIWDY

LOFUND

Good,
I'm beat

I got
it

AFTER WORKING ALL NIGHT TO SOLVE THE COMPUTER GLITCH IT---

Now arrange the circled letters to form the surprise answer, as suggested by the above cartoon.

Print answer here "⬡⬡⬡⬡⬡⬡" ON ⬡⬡⬡

JUMBLE

Unscramble these four Jumbles, one letter to each square, to form four ordinary words.

OXUMB

INSIF

NOCTRE

STOFFE

This will be a "meaty" item

WHAT IT WAS WORTH WHEN THE MOVIE HUNK POSED IN A SKIMPY SWIMSUIT.

Now arrange the circled letters to form the surprise answer, as suggested by the above cartoon.

Print answer here A "〇〇〇〇〇" 〇〇〇〇〇〇〇

JUMBLE®

Unscramble these four Jumbles, one letter to each square, to form four ordinary words.

ENTAK

OYLED

UNROAD

ZARABA

Guess it's my night, boys

WHEN THE GARDENER WON THE HIGH-STAKES POKER HAND, HE----

Now arrange the circled letters to form the surprise answer, as suggested by the above cartoon.

Print answer here " ⟨◯◯◯◯◯⟩ " IN A ⟨◯◯◯◯◯◯⟩

JUMBLE.

Unscramble these four Jumbles, one letter to each square, to form four ordinary words.

EYAPE

SOMYS

FUPULC

MEEDAF

WHAT THE NEIGHBORS DID WHEN THE SMOKE-BELCHING JALOPY DROVE BY.

Now arrange the circled letters to form the surprise answer, as suggested by the above cartoon.

Print answer here " ⬡⬡⬡⬡⬡ "

JUMBLE®

Unscramble these four Jumbles, one letter to each square, to form four ordinary words.

INGGA

YUMST

CEETIX

CHOBOR

It's too hot with my coat on

GR-R-INK

WHAT THE EXOTIC DANCER STRIPPED WHILE SHE DROVE.

Now arrange the circled letters to form the surprise answer, as suggested by the above cartoon.

Print answer here

JUMBLE®

Unscramble these four Jumbles, one letter to each square, to form four ordinary words.

HYATS

KOSTE

WEABER

ENCOSH

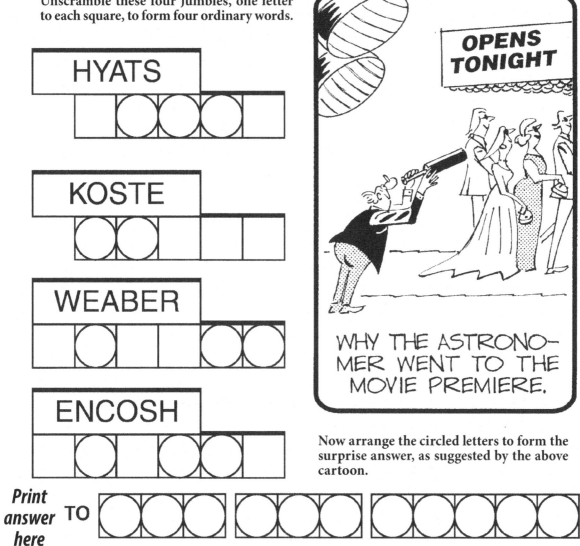

OPENS TONIGHT

WHY THE ASTRONO-MER WENT TO THE MOVIE PREMIERE.

Now arrange the circled letters to form the surprise answer, as suggested by the above cartoon.

Print answer here TO ☐☐☐ ☐☐☐ ☐☐☐☐☐

JUMBLE®

Unscramble these four Jumbles, one letter to each square, to form four ordinary words.

INWET

DIXEO

CEADDE

YERRSH

It's freezing in here, you tightwad

Pay the rent, you deadbeat

A COLD APARTMENT CAN LEAD TO THIS.

Now arrange the circled letters to form the surprise answer, as suggested by the above cartoon.

Print answer here " ⬡⬡⬡⬡⬡⬡ " ⬡⬡⬡⬡⬡

JUMBLE®

Unscramble these four Jumbles, one letter to each square, to form four ordinary words.

OGGRE

UDTNE

UNBART

DIMROB

...and then he winked at her and said...

WHAT A PRISSY MATRON MIGHT DO WHEN TOLD AN OFF-COLOR JOKE.

Now arrange the circled letters to form the surprise answer, as suggested by the above cartoon.

Print answer here

JUMBLE®

Unscramble these four Jumbles, one letter to each square, to form four ordinary words.

KALOC

WOLLY

LABBED

RUSTYD

He never falls asleep on the job

WHAT A NIGHT WATCHMAN NEVER DOES.

Now arrange the circled letters to form the surprise answer, as suggested by the above cartoon.

Print answer here A ⬡⬡⬡ ' ⬡ ⬡⬡⬡⬡⬡

JUMBLE

Unscramble these four Jumbles, one letter to each square, to form four ordinary words.

FERAT

TIFED

BEEVAH

YARTTE

Slow down, this isn't a race

I need to learn to relax

WHY THE DRAG RACER TOOK GOLF LESSONS.

Now arrange the circled letters to form the surprise answer, as suggested by the above cartoon.

Print answer here TO " ◯◯◯◯◯ " ◯◯◯◯◯◯

JUMBLE®

Unscramble these four Jumbles, one letter to each square, to form four ordinary words.

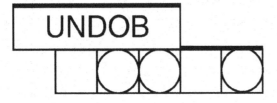
UNDOB

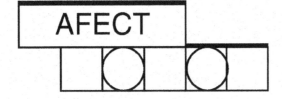
AFECT

NIRBON

SIGAHR

They love
to play

They
sure
are
frisky

WHAT THE COLTS
LIKED TO DO.

Now arrange the circled letters to form the surprise answer, as suggested by the above cartoon.

Print
answer
here

JUMBLE

Unscramble these four Jumbles, one letter to each square, to form four ordinary words.

RODLE

VOYCE

BAHCLE

TAMMOR

WHEN HE TOOK THE DEEP-SEA-DIVING TEST, HE WAS IN----

Now arrange the circled letters to form the surprise answer, as suggested by the above cartoon.

Print answer here ⬡⬡⬡⬡ **HIS** ⬡⬡⬡⬡

JUMBLE®

Unscramble these four Jumbles, one letter
to each square, to form four ordinary words.

SUIGE

FREVE

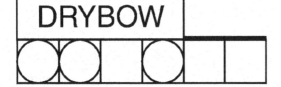

DRYBOW

GLAHGE

Let's go home, Nellie. I can hardly talk   SCRAM!

HOW THE CARRIAGE DRIVER FELT WHEN HE CAUGHT A COLD.

Now arrange the circled letters to form the
surprise answer, as suggested by the above
cartoon.

Print answer here ⬭⬭⬭⬭⬭⬭ **AND** ⬭⬭⬭⬭⬭

JUMBLE®

Unscramble these four Jumbles, one letter to each square, to form four ordinary words.

DIOTT

TAFOO

CORTER

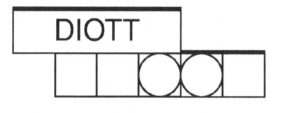

GLINSE

But I only called my girlfriend

473 times?!

WHAT JUNIOR GOT WHEN THE CELL PHONE BILL ARRIVED.

Now arrange the circled letters to form the surprise answer, as suggested by the above cartoon.

Print answer here A  OF " "

JUMBLE®

Unscramble these four Jumbles, one letter to each square, to form four ordinary words.

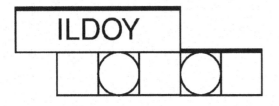

ILDOY

TWAHR

ENFADE

THUGOR

Joyce Kilmer was right

A GOOD THING TO DO BEFORE BUY- ING A BOOK ON TREES.

Now arrange the circled letters to form the surprise answer, as suggested by the above cartoon.

Print answer here " ☐☐☐☐☐ " ☐☐☐☐☐☐☐ IT

JUMBLE

Unscramble these four Jumbles, one letter to each square, to form four ordinary words.

PIRAD

SARBS

LADVAN

KLAYEC

Harry, wake up, this is the ending

WHERE THE FAT LADY SINGS AT THE OPERA.

Now arrange the circled letters to form the surprise answer, as suggested by the above cartoon.

Print answer here THE ⬡⬡⬡⬡⬡ ⬡⬡⬡⬡

JUMBLE®

Unscramble these four Jumbles, one letter
to each square, to form four ordinary words.

MYTEP

SAYES

KLYFNU

YABSUW

This one's
a cinch

WHAT THE BUSY
PICKPOCKET LIKED
TO DO.

Now arrange the circled letters to form the
surprise answer, as suggested by the above
cartoon.

Print answer here ⭕⭕⭕⭕ IT " ⭕⭕⭕⭕ "

JUMBLE®

Unscramble these four Jumbles, one letter to each square, to form four ordinary words.

BANIC
◯ □ □ □ □

BYGAG
□ □ □ □ ◯

SYVURC
□ □ ◯ □ □ □

SAQUEY
□ □ □ ◯ ◯ □

Want some gravy, darlin'?

HOW HE DESCRIBED THE WAITRESS' REMARKS.

Now arrange the circled letters to form the surprise answer, as suggested by the above cartoon.

Print answer here " ◯ ◯ ◯ ◯ ◯ "

JUMBLE®

Unscramble these four Jumbles, one letter
to each square, to form four ordinary words.

TILOP

DEHIC

VYCOON

PREDON

She's
a fake

She told
me I'd
be married
by now

WHEN THE SEER'S
SERVICES DIDN'T
SELL AT THE
CHARITY AUCTION,
SHE BECAME---

Now arrange the circled letters to form the
surprise answer, as suggested by the above
cartoon.

Print
answer
here

A ◯◯◯ - ◯◯◯◯◯◯◯

JUMBLE

Unscramble these four Jumbles, one letter to each square, to form four ordinary words.

ANSPY

WYSON

VIRTED

OSUREA

The champ was the odds-on favorite

How could I lose?

WHEN THE TENNIS CHAMP LOST TO THE AMATEUR, HE---

Now arrange the circled letters to form the surprise answer, as suggested by the above cartoon.

Print answer here " "

25

JUMBLE®

Unscramble these four Jumbles, one letter to each square, to form four ordinary words.

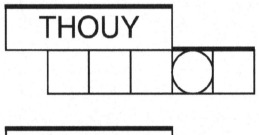

THOUY

PHULS

GONNIG

WEENST

Good morning, Mrs. Flegelhommer

Have a nice day, Mr. Briteglass

HE WAS A GOOD DOORMAN BECAUSE HE KNEW THE----

Now arrange the circled letters to form the surprise answer, as suggested by the above cartoon.

Print answer here

 AND

Rainy Day JUMBLE®

Daily Puzzles

JUMBLE®

Unscramble these four Jumbles, one letter to each square, to form four ordinary words.

RUJOR

ISTUE

LOSTCY

ROTHEX

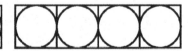

No, no! If you take Fourth Street to Grand you'll save 10 minutes

THE BARBER WAS GOOD AT THIS.

Now arrange the circled letters to form the surprise answer, as suggested by the above cartoon.

Print answer here

JUMBLE®

Unscramble these four Jumbles, one letter to each square, to form four ordinary words.

VILIC

CAUDT

HIRSLE

PARMEC

For you, I'm charging choice for the prime cut

WHAT THE BUTCHER DID FOR HIS GOOD CUSTOMER.

Now arrange the circled letters to form the surprise answer, as suggested by the above cartoon.

Print answer here "⬡⬡⬡⬡⬡⬡" THE ⬡⬡⬡⬡⬡

JUMBLE®

Unscramble these four Jumbles, one letter
to each square, to form four ordinary words.

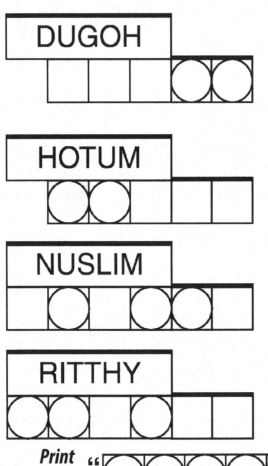

DUGOH

HOTUM

NUSLIM

RITTHY

Our monthly
bill will
be lower

Yippee, only
10 hours
'til sunup

THIS HELPED TO
PASS THE TIME
WHEN THE POWER
WENT OUT.

Now arrange the circled letters to form the
surprise answer, as suggested by the above
cartoon.

Print
answer
here

JUMBLE®

Unscramble these four Jumbles, one letter to each square, to form four ordinary words.

CORFE

VELED

DEWIST

FORLEG

It's a nice face, a kind one, a little worn, maybe, but...

AFTER HE HUNG THE MIRROR, HE---

Now arrange the circled letters to form the surprise answer, as suggested by the above cartoon.

Print answer here " ☐☐☐☐☐☐☐☐☐ " **ON IT**

JUMBLE

Unscramble these four Jumbles, one letter
to each square, to form four ordinary words.

FLAUW

VOLEN

WORDSY

CLUDED

All in a
row, boys

Of all
the luck

WHEN THE ARTIST
WON THE POKER
HAND, THE LOSERS
SAID HE---

Now arrange the circled letters to form the
surprise answer, as suggested by the above
cartoon.

Print answer here " ◯◯◯◯ " ◯◯◯◯

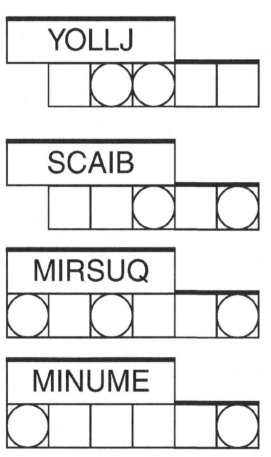

Unscramble these four Jumbles, one letter to each square, to form four ordinary words.

YOLLJ

SCAIB

MIRSUQ

MINUME

WHAT THE SHOE-MAKER LISTENED TO WHILE HE WORKED.

Now arrange the circled letters to form the surprise answer, as suggested by the above cartoon.

Print answer here " ◯◯◯◯ " ◯◯◯◯◯◯

JUMBLE®

Unscramble these four Jumbles, one letter to each square, to form four ordinary words.

PYLAP

UNAFA

HIRDBY

DELIJA

Keep 'em coming

We got it now

WHEN THE BUCKET BRIGADE FOUGHT THE BLAZE, THEY WERE---

Now arrange the circled letters to form the surprise answer, as suggested by the above cartoon.

Print answer here ALL "◯◯◯◯◯" ◯◯

JUMBLE®

Unscramble these four Jumbles, one letter to each square, to form four ordinary words.

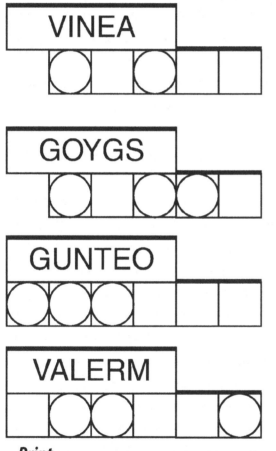

VINEA

GOYGS

GUNTEO

VALERM

We're through. You'll never settle down

But what about the good times?

SHE DUMPED THE GUITARIST BECAUSE HE WANTED TO---

Now arrange the circled letters to form the surprise answer, as suggested by the above cartoon.

Print answer here "◯◯◯◯◯◯" HER ◯◯◯◯◯

JUMBLE

Unscramble these four Jumbles, one letter
to each square, to form four ordinary words.

DUGAY

LAMDY

VACIDE

TRAWEY

Those uphill
turns are
scary

You
did
fine

WHEN THE TRUCKER
PASSED THE MOUNT-
AIN DRIVING TEST,
HE----

Now arrange the circled letters to form the
surprise answer, as suggested by the above
cartoon.

Print answer here

THE " "

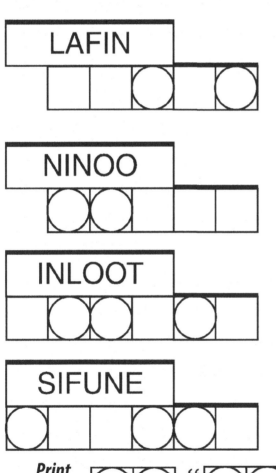

Unscramble these four Jumbles, one letter
to each square, to form four ordinary words.

LAFIN

NINOO

INLOOT

SIFUNE

Only half done and I
can't get to the store

WHAT MOM FACED
WHEN SHE RAN OUT
OF WINDOW
CLEANER.

Now arrange the circled letters to form the
surprise answer, as suggested by the above
cartoon.

*Print
answer
here*

" "

JUMBLE®

Unscramble these four Jumbles, one letter
to each square, to form four ordinary words.

CYKAT

NAYRE

THINEZ

RETAIS

I've got to get out
of here. I'm going nuts

HOW THE BAKER
FELT AFTER
MAKING CAKES
ALL DAY.

Now arrange the circled letters to form the
surprise answer, as suggested by the above
cartoon.

Print answer here "  "

JUMBLE

Unscramble these four Jumbles, one letter to each square, to form four ordinary words.

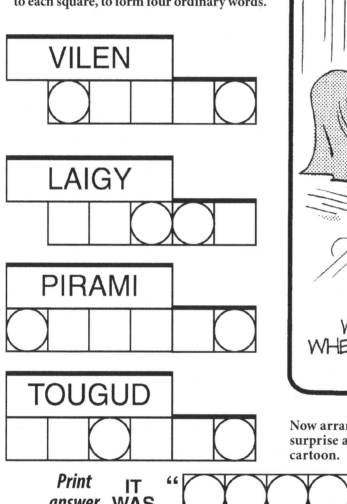

VILEN

LAIGY

PIRAMI

TOUGUD

She hit notes even a songbird can't reach

WHAT HE SAID WHEN THE CONCERT WAS OVER.

Now arrange the circled letters to form the surprise answer, as suggested by the above cartoon.

Print answer here IT WAS " ⃝⃝⃝⃝⃝⃝⃝⃝⃝⃝ "

JUMBLE®

Unscramble these four Jumbles, one letter
to each square, to form four ordinary words.

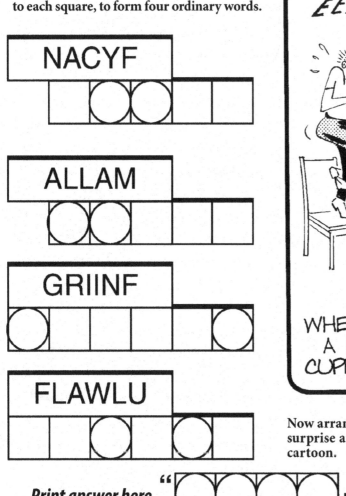

NACYF

ALLAM

GRIINF

FLAWLU

EEK— It ate through the cereal box

WHEN SHE SPOTTED A MOUSE IN THE CUPBOARD, IT WAS——

Now arrange the circled letters to form the
surprise answer, as suggested by the above
cartoon.

Print answer here " ☐☐☐☐☐ - ☐☐☐☐☐ "

JUMBLE®

Unscramble these four Jumbles, one letter to each square, to form four ordinary words.

CATUE

HYBUS

NYFLOD

DEGURT

THIS CAR IS LIKE A LENGTHY PRISON TERM BECAUSE THEY'RE BOTH----

Now arrange the circled letters to form the surprise answer, as suggested by the above cartoon.

Print answer here A ⬡⬡⬡⬡ "⬡⬡⬡⬡⬡⬡⬡"

JUMBLE®

Unscramble these four Jumbles, one letter to each square, to form four ordinary words.

UGGOE

RUIFT

CLINEP

NOIDIE

You look terrific

Tonight's the big night

WHERE SHE WENT BEFORE THE HIGH SCHOOL REUNION.

Now arrange the circled letters to form the surprise answer, as suggested by the above cartoon.

Print answer here ◯◯ A ◯◯◯◯◯

JUMBLE®

Unscramble these four Jumbles, one letter
to each square, to form four ordinary words.

DOLDY

TADPA

CADAFE

GYLINK

More efficiency,
less stress

Too much
money, too
little return

WHEN THE EXECU-
TIVE ASKED THE
BOARD FOR A
COMPANY PLANE,
HIS REQUEST——

Now arrange the circled letters to form the
surprise answer, as suggested by the above
cartoon.

Print answer here ◯◯◯◯ '◯ "◯◯◯"

JUMBLE®

Unscramble these four Jumbles, one letter to each square, to form four ordinary words.

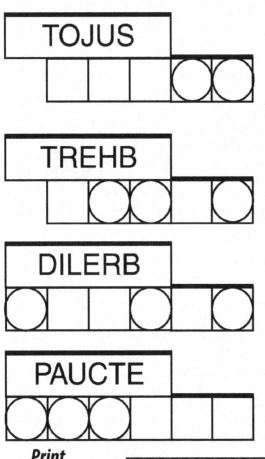

TOJUS

TREHB

DILERB

PAUCTE

This will give you more protection

SHE BOUGHT THE PRICEY SUNSCREEN BECAUSE IT WAS---

Now arrange the circled letters to form the surprise answer, as suggested by the above cartoon.

Print answer here A " ◯◯◯◯◯ " ◯◯◯◯◯◯

JUMBLE®

Unscramble these four Jumbles, one letter to each square, to form four ordinary words.

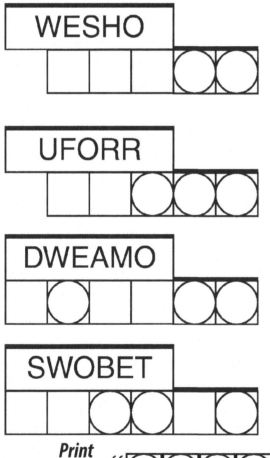

WESHO

UFORR

DWEAMO

SWOBET

I'll take a pound of these, a pound of those, and...

I really miss chocolate

EASY TO EXPERIENCE ON A SUGAR-FREE DIET.

Now arrange the circled letters to form the surprise answer, as suggested by the above cartoon.

Print answer here " ⃝⃝⃝⃝⃝ " ⃝⃝⃝⃝⃝⃝

JUMBLE®

Unscramble these four Jumbles, one letter
to each square, to form four ordinary words.

YARAR

GOMOR

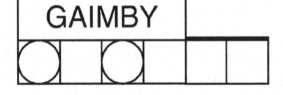

GAIMBY

NULKIE

No place
to go

Nothing
to do

WHY HE QUIT
HIS JOB ON THE
OFFSHORE OIL
RIG.

Now arrange the circled letters to form the
surprise answer, as suggested by the above
cartoon.

Print answer here   IT WAS " 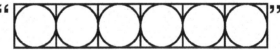 "

JUMBLE

Unscramble these four Jumbles, one letter
to each square, to form four ordinary words.

GEMAL

DOBOL

HATHEL

REWEPT

I'd rather get
a new pair

SHOE
REPAIR
SHOP

50%
OFF

My boots
are fine

THE SOCIETY
MATRONS PASSED
UP THE SHOE-REPAIR
OFFER BECAUSE
THEY WERE——

Now arrange the circled letters to form the
surprise answer, as suggested by the above
cartoon.

*Print
answer
here*

" "

47

JUMBLE®

Unscramble these four Jumbles, one letter to each square, to form four ordinary words.

DIATS

EPPIR

STUCCA

KUSTEM

Four touchdowns in a row

He's going to be a star

COACH

WHY THE YOUNG QUARTERBACK MADE THE VARSITY TEAM.

Now arrange the circled letters to form the surprise answer, as suggested by the above cartoon.

Print answer here   HE "◯◯◯◯◯◯◯" THE ◯◯◯◯◯

JUMBLE®

Unscramble these four Jumbles, one letter to each square, to form four ordinary words.

MERIG

GERAW

NARLAC

REFTER

Free health care for everyone

You should run for office

WHERE THE HOCKEY PLAYER WITH LIBERAL VIEWS PLAYED.

Now arrange the circled letters to form the surprise answer, as suggested by the above cartoon.

Print answer here AT " ⬡⬡⬡⬡ " ⬡⬡⬡⬡

JUMBLE®

Unscramble these four Jumbles, one letter to each square, to form four ordinary words.

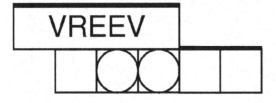

VREEV

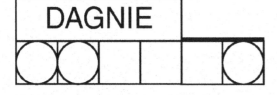

KNITH

DAGNIE

SLIMAD

Ughh, this is awful!

The directions were difficult to follow

A COMPLEX RECIPE CAN BE THIS.

Now arrange the circled letters to form the surprise answer, as suggested by the above cartoon.

Print answer here

 TO "  "

JUMBLE®

Unscramble these four Jumbles, one letter to each square, to form four ordinary words.

MEZIA

DAKEB

OFTROG

PERICH

HONEST SAM'S USED CARS

It runs like new, trust me!

WHAT THE SHADY SALESMAN DID TO THE UNSUSPECTING BUYER.

Now arrange the circled letters to form the surprise answer, as suggested by the above cartoon.

Print answer here

 FOR A

JUMBLE®

Unscramble these four Jumbles, one letter to each square, to form four ordinary words.

BYMUP

LEREC

SEJERY

GOURAC

Nice job, Snedly

Let's talk about my commission

$40,000

WHEN THE RING SOLD FOR A PREMIUM PRICE, THE JEWELER SAID IT WAS A ————

Now arrange the circled letters to form the surprise answer, as suggested by the above cartoon.

Print answer here " ◯◯◯ " OF A ◯◯◯◯

JUMBLE®

Unscramble these four Jumbles, one letter to each square, to form four ordinary words.

GOUBS

TOMIF

ZEFRYN

RAUBUE

This is tougher than riding a horse

WHAT THE JOCKEY ENJOYED.

Now arrange the circled letters to form the surprise answer, as suggested by the above cartoon.

Print answer here  AND

JUMBLE®

Unscramble these four Jumbles, one letter to each square, to form four ordinary words.

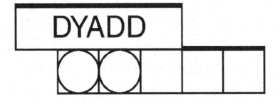

DYADD

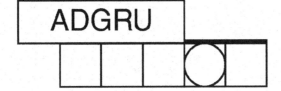

ADGRU

VANGER

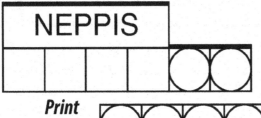

NEPPIS

Just buy a
new pair

HE HAD A
HOLE IN HIS
SOCK BECAUSE
HIS WIFE
DIDN'T ---

Now arrange the circled letters to form the surprise answer, as suggested by the above cartoon.

Print answer here ⬭⬭⬭⬭ A " ⬭⬭⬭⬭ "

JUMBLE

Unscramble these four Jumbles, one letter to each square, to form four ordinary words.

JONEY

GANTE

TABLLE

DRIZAW

WHAT THE TEEN SAID WHEN HIS YOUNGER BROTHER PLAYED HIS DRUMS.

Now arrange the circled letters to form the surprise answer, as suggested by the above cartoon.

Print answer here " ⬡⬡⬡⬡ ⬡⬡ "

JUMBLE®

Unscramble these four Jumbles, one letter
to each square, to form four ordinary words.

TILUQ

GLOIC

NEPTLY

DARAPE

If you had two cookies
and I gave you two more,
how many would you have?

1,2,3
Let's
see...

HOW THE CHILDREN
LEARNED TO ADD
BEFORE COM-
PUTERS.

Now arrange the circled letters to form the
surprise answer, as suggested by the above
cartoon.

Print answer here " "

JUMBLE

Unscramble these four Jumbles, one letter to each square, to form four ordinary words.

FONTE

ROCUS

YORPET

NEPAHP

See? It comes right back

WHEN HE GOT A BOOMERANG FOR HIS BIRTH-DAY, HE ENJOYED MANY---

Now arrange the circled letters to form the surprise answer, as suggested by the above cartoon.

Print answer here

57

JUMBLE®

Unscramble these four Jumbles, one letter to each square, to form four ordinary words.

CHULG

NOAGY

SOPHIL

HESTIF

You're on your own

Up, up, and away, into the wild blue yonder

WHAT THE INSTRUCTOR INSISTED ON WHEN THE SINGER WANTED TO BE A PILOT.

Now arrange the circled letters to form the surprise answer, as suggested by the above cartoon.

Print answer here

A " ⬭⬭⬭⬭ " ⬭⬭⬭⬭⬭⬭

58

JUMBLE

Unscramble these four Jumbles, one letter
to each square, to form four ordinary words.

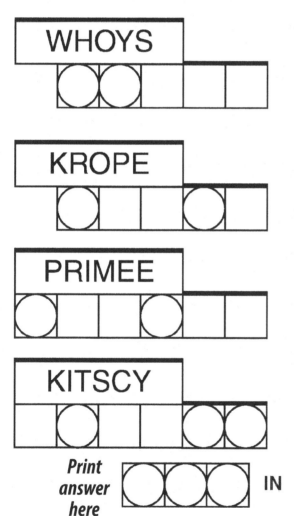

WHOYS

KROPE

PRIMEE

KITSCY

I need your donations. I'll
fight for better schools,
better roads...

VOTE FOR
HONEST
ERNEST

WHAT YOU CAN
END UP WITH
WHEN A CANDI-
DATE ASKS
FOR "DOUGH".

Now arrange the circled letters to form the
surprise answer, as suggested by the above
cartoon.

Print
answer
here

IN

JUMBLE®

Unscramble these four Jumbles, one letter
to each square, to form four ordinary words.

ONLOY

WANTY

CROUTY

ERROBB

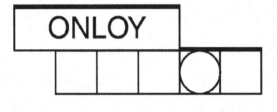

All I want to do is get
into my pajamas

HOW SHE FELT
AFTER MODELING
CLOTHES ALL
DAY.

Now arrange the circled letters to form the
surprise answer, as suggested by the above
cartoon.

Print answer here " 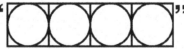 "

JUMBLE®

Unscramble these four Jumbles, one letter to each square, to form four ordinary words.

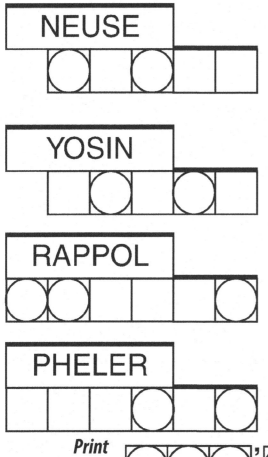

NEUSE

YOSIN

RAPPOL

PHELER

It's not how you drive, it's how you arrive

WHAT THE CHAMPION GOLFER OFFERED HIS AMATEUR PARTNERS.

Now arrange the circled letters to form the surprise answer, as suggested by the above cartoon.

Print answer here

JUMBLE

Unscramble these four Jumbles, one letter to each square, to form four ordinary words.

NLFAK

STULY

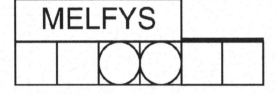

MELFYS

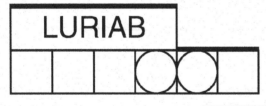

LURIAB

I need a spinnaker

You're in luck. They're 20% off this week

WHAT THE YACHTS-MAN FOUND AT THE BOAT SHOP.

Now arrange the circled letters to form the surprise answer, as suggested by the above cartoon.

Print answer here A ◯◯◯◯ ◯◯◯◯

JUMBLE®

Unscramble these four Jumbles, one letter to each square, to form four ordinary words.

EAGAD

VALEG

SLUDON

USEBUD

Oops! Dropped another one

DRINKING BEER WHILE PLAYING PICNIC BASEBALL CAN LEAD TO THIS.

Now arrange the circled letters to form the surprise answer, as suggested by the above cartoon.

Print answer here

" "

JUMBLE®

Unscramble these four Jumbles, one letter to each square, to form four ordinary words.

SNALT

LANVA

YELLIK

MYTIES

WHAT MOM MADE WHEN THE FIRST-GRADER CAME HOME FROM CLASS.

Now arrange the circled letters to form the surprise answer, as suggested by the above cartoon.

Print answer here " ☐☐☐☐☐ " ☐☐☐☐

Unscramble these four Jumbles, one letter to each square, to form four ordinary words.

TRIDY

TYJET

SARROY

BEMFUL

She dresses like a businesswoman

Straight As

WHAT THE VALE-DICTORIAN WORE TO HER INTER-VIEW FOR COLLEGE.

Now arrange the circled letters to form the surprise answer, as suggested by the above cartoon.

Print answer here

A " _____ " _____

JUMBLE®

Unscramble these four Jumbles, one letter to each square, to form four ordinary words.

YIXST

EDDIC

NOMCOM

JELGAN

10:00 tee time. I can't let down the guys

WHEN DAD DIDN'T HELP WITH THE CARPET CLEANING, MOM WAS ----

Now arrange the circled letters to form the surprise answer, as suggested by the above cartoon.

Print answer here "⚪⚪⚪⚪⚪⚪⚪⚪"

66

JUMBLE

Unscramble these four Jumbles, one letter to each square, to form four ordinary words.

GULAH

CUIJE

LIERIX

INKELT

Inconsiderate #$%***?@**!!

I'm calling the police

WHAT THE COUPLE DID WHEN THE UPSTAIRS NEIGHBORS HAD A DANCE PARTY.

Now arrange the circled letters to form the surprise answer, as suggested by the above cartoon.

Print answer here " ⬭⬭⬭ " THE ⬭⬭⬭⬭⬭⬭⬭

JUMBLE

Unscramble these four Jumbles, one letter to each square, to form four ordinary words.

HOPOW

WENYL

DALINS

NOBBOA

Wow! That's huge

I've got to get some photos

WHEN THE TOR-
NADO HUNTERS
SPOTTED THE
TWISTER, THEY
WERE----

Now arrange the circled letters to form the surprise answer, as suggested by the above cartoon.

Print answer here "◯◯◯◯◯" ◯◯◯◯

JUMBLE

Unscramble these four Jumbles, one letter to each square, to form four ordinary words.

MEVON

RIMEN

RAMAAD

FACTUE

Now I can hang this up and really study it

WHAT THE DOCTOR ESTABLISHED WHEN HE MOUNTED A DIAGRAM OF THE BRAIN.

Now arrange the circled letters to form the surprise answer, as suggested by the above cartoon.

Print answer here

A " ⬡⬡⬡⬡⬡ " OF ⬡⬡⬡⬡

JUMBLE®

Unscramble these four Jumbles, one letter to each square, to form four ordinary words.

LAWRC

MOAXI

PHEWEN

BONYED

Late again, Higgins. We may not need you anymore

Restaurant was crowded

PRESIDENT

WHEN HE TOOK TOO MANY LUNCHES, HE BECAME----

Now arrange the circled letters to form the surprise answer, as suggested by the above cartoon.

Print answer here " "

JUMBLE®

Unscramble these four Jumbles, one letter
to each square, to form four ordinary words.

TINFE

ICCOL

SCOMAT

SHAMON

He never gives
a fair grade

Let's
sue

WHAT THE LAW
PROFESSOR FACED
WHEN THE STUDENTS
PROTESTED.

Now arrange the circled letters to form the
surprise answer, as suggested by the above
cartoon.

Print
answer
here

A " ⬡⬡⬡⬡⬡ " ⬡⬡⬡⬡⬡⬡

JUMBLE

Unscramble these four Jumbles, one letter to each square, to form four ordinary words.

NUNAL

ROGUD

TELKET

BOLTAC

Yes, he's a good risk for a large loan

THE BANKER HIRED THE SEER BECAUSE HE NEEDED----

Now arrange the circled letters to form the surprise answer, as suggested by the above cartoon.

Print answer here A " ⃝⃝⃝⃝⃝⃝ "

PUZZLE
71

JUMBLE

Unscramble these four Jumbles, one letter to each square, to form four ordinary words.

POURC

BALOT

DEFAUL

TRUSEY

I'll take a dozen long-stems

Me too

I need a table spread

WHAT THE FLORIST FACED WHEN BUSI-NESS IMPROVED.

Now arrange the circled letters to form the surprise answer, as suggested by the above cartoon.

Print answer here A " ◯◯◯◯ " ◯◯◯◯◯◯◯

73

JUMBLE.

Unscramble these four Jumbles, one letter to each square, to form four ordinary words.

PARVO

NARCK

KUBECT

IPSOME

Quick, grab the umbrellas

WHEN CLOUDS FORMED OVER THE OPEN-AIR THEATER THE ACTOR SAID----

Now arrange the circled letters to form the surprise answer, as suggested by the above cartoon.

Print answer here   IT'S ⬡⬡⬡⬡ "⬡⬡⬡⬡"

JUMBLE®

Unscramble these four Jumbles, one letter to each square, to form four ordinary words.

YURLT

CRAHN

TUNBOY

GIBNEN

You did it, now admit it

Who, me?

WHAT THE COPS DEMANDED FROM THE ARSON SUSPECT.

Now arrange the circled letters to form the surprise answer, as suggested by the above cartoon.

Print answer here

THE "☐☐☐☐☐☐☐" ☐☐☐☐☐

JUMBLE®

Unscramble these four Jumbles, one letter
to each square, to form four ordinary words.

FIRRA

PIPNY

STOJEL

TANIAT

AIR
75¢

I used to
get it free

WHEN GRAMPS PAID
TO FILL HIS
TIRES WITH AIR,
HE CONSIDERED IT—

Now arrange the circled letters to form the
surprise answer, as suggested by the above
cartoon.

Print answer here " ◯◯◯◯◯◯◯◯◯ "

76

JUMBLE®

Unscramble these four Jumbles, one letter to each square, to form four ordinary words.

NOJIT

EBOES

SHORUC

MASALB

Put 'em in the back

WHERE THE CON-
DUCTOR PLACED THE
OFFICERS IN THE
MILITARY
ORCHESTRA.

Now arrange the circled letters to form the surprise answer, as suggested by the above cartoon.

Print answer here THE " ⬡⬡⬡⬡⬡ " ⬡⬡⬡⬡⬡⬡⬡

JUMBLE®

Unscramble these four Jumbles, one letter to each square, to form four ordinary words.

DEGIM

KAQUE

WARBOR

PROTTE

You've got two meetings and the sales report is due

I'm ready for a nap

TOUGH TO DO AFTER A WORKOUT.

Now arrange the circled letters to form the surprise answer, as suggested by the above cartoon.

Print answer here

⬡⬡⬡ THE ⬡⬡⬡⬡ ⬡⬡⬡

JUMBLE®

Unscramble these four Jumbles, one letter
to each square, to form four ordinary words.

HAIKK

JABON

YULIBS

TENSOX

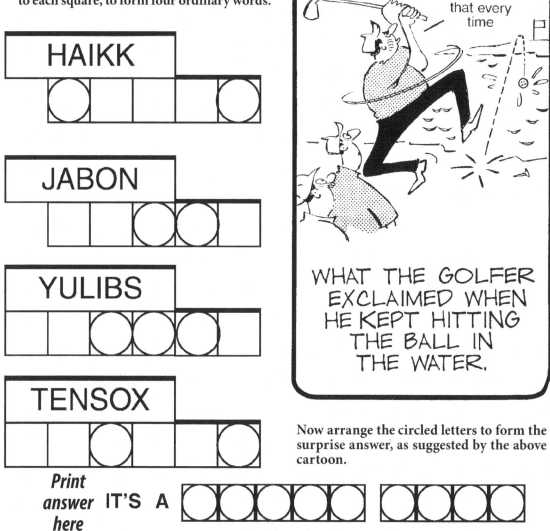

#%*!!! I do
that every
time

WHAT THE GOLFER
EXCLAIMED WHEN
HE KEPT HITTING
THE BALL IN
THE WATER.

Now arrange the circled letters to form the
surprise answer, as suggested by the above
cartoon.

*Print
answer
here* IT'S A ☐☐☐☐☐ ☐☐☐☐

JUMBLE®

Unscramble these four Jumbles, one letter to each square, to form four ordinary words.

RABDN

JEDDA

ABAANN

RASTUX

KEEP OFF

Glad, we're not up there

THE MUSICIANS DIDN'T USE THE RICKETY PLATFORM BECAUSE IT WAS----

Now arrange the circled letters to form the surprise answer, as suggested by the above cartoon.

Print answer here   A   " ◯◯◯◯◯◯ " ◯◯◯◯◯

JUMBLE

Unscramble these four Jumbles, one letter to each square, to form four ordinary words.

NOSOW

PYKER

TEPICS

CALKAJ

He looks like a movie star and he's so nice

I saw him first

WHEN SHE WAS "TAKEN" BY HER FRIEND'S BEAU, SHE WAS REMINDED THAT HE----

Now arrange the circled letters to form the surprise answer, as suggested by the above cartoon.

Print answer here

"   "

JUMBLE®

Unscramble these four Jumbles, one letter to each square, to form four ordinary words.

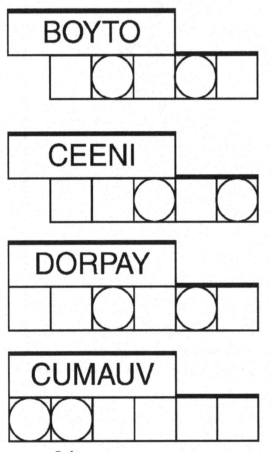

BOYTO

CEENI

DORPAY

CUMAUV

BONG   Thanks for a lovely time

WHAT HE REALIZED WHEN SHE DECLINED THE KISS AT MID-NIGHT.

Now arrange the circled letters to form the surprise answer, as suggested by the above cartoon.

Print answer here   THE " ◯◯◯◯ " WAS ◯◯◯◯

JUMBLE®

Unscramble these four Jumbles, one letter to each square, to form four ordinary words.

LAWRD

TEABA

BUSTIM

KELNER

He said it would go to 50. It went to five.

WALL ST.

STOCKS

WHEN THE ANALYST'S FORE-CAST FELL SHORT, THE INVESTOR REALIZED IT WAS---

Now arrange the circled letters to form the surprise answer, as suggested by the above cartoon.

Print answer here

" ⬤⬤⬤⬤ " ⬤⬤⬤⬤⬤⬤

JUMBLE

Unscramble these four Jumbles, one letter
to each square, to form four ordinary words.

NAGLD

WILLT

CLISHE

RETULB

What's a big movie
star like you
doing here?

I volunteer
every
Thursday

HOW THE REPORTER
GOT A SCOOP AT
THE SOUP KITCHEN.

Now arrange the circled letters to form the
surprise answer, as suggested by the above
cartoon.

Print answer here ◯◯◯◯ A ◯◯◯◯◯◯

JUMBLE®

Unscramble these four Jumbles, one letter to each square, to form four ordinary words.

NYLAM

NAIPO

YARBEN

SPUGMY

That'll be $50

There go my winnings

HOW THE BOWLER PAID FOR THE ACUPUNCTURE TREATMENT.

Now arrange the circled letters to form the surprise answer, as suggested by the above cartoon.

Print answer here WITH " ⬡⬡⬡ " ⬡⬡⬡⬡⬡

JUMBLE®

Unscramble these four Jumbles, one letter to each square, to form four ordinary words.

FIRGE

TOISH

HERVIT

MIRADS

Good! That'll fix that loudmouth

WHAT THE TEN-NIS FANS SAID WHEN HE ACED THE OBNOXIOUS FAVORITE.

Now arrange the circled letters to form the surprise answer, as suggested by the above cartoon.

Print answer here " ◯◯◯◯◯◯◯ " HIM ◯◯◯◯◯

JUMBLE

Unscramble these four Jumbles, one letter
to each square, to form four ordinary words.

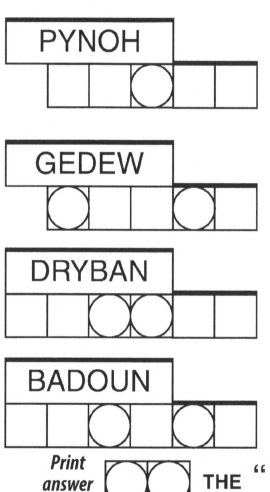

PYNOH

GEDEW

DRYBAN

BADOUN

Stay with
the buckboard

THE COWBOY
DIDN'T JOIN HIS
PALS IN THE
SALOON BECAUSE
HE WAS----

Now arrange the circled letters to form the
surprise answer, as suggested by the above
cartoon.

Print
answer
here

THE "   "

JUMBLE

Unscramble these four Jumbles, one letter
to each square, to form four ordinary words.

BUAQS

CONOR

IROING

BLIGET

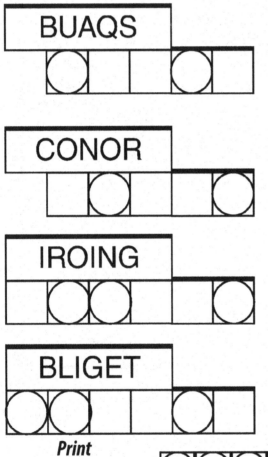

I guess we'll
just order out

WHAT THE KING
SAID WHEN THE
STORM RUINED HIS
PICNIC PLANS.

Now arrange the circled letters to form the
surprise answer, as suggested by the above
cartoon.

Print
answer THE
here

88

JUMBLE®

Unscramble these four Jumbles, one letter to each square, to form four ordinary words.

LORGY

FODOL

UNBRAU

CLYMAL

...and then her son found her

Oh, that's beautiful

WHY THE KNITTING GROUP INVITED THE STORYTELLER.

Now arrange the circled letters to form the surprise answer, as suggested by the above cartoon.

Print answer here FOR A ⬜⬜⬜⬜ " ⬜⬜⬜⬜ "

JUMBLE®

Unscramble these four Jumbles, one letter to each square, to form four ordinary words.

LEBEL

MYDUP

KEPPUE

DISPUT

I'll have it fixed in no time

It's very dark

WHAT HE DID WHEN THE CEILING LIGHT FAILED.

Now arrange the circled letters to form the surprise answer, as suggested by the above cartoon.

Print answer here " ☐☐☐☐☐☐☐ " ☐☐

JUMBLE®

Unscramble these four Jumbles, one letter
to each square, to form four ordinary words.

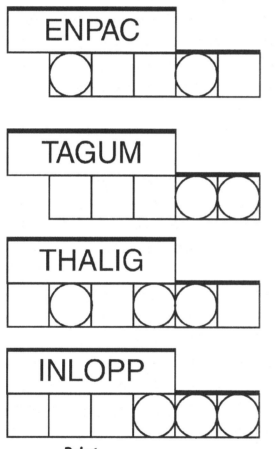

ENPAC

TAGUM

THALIG

INLOPP

But Sarge, what
if I fall?

WHEN THE
RECRUIT WAS
ASSIGNED A TOP
BUNK, HE WAS----

Now arrange the circled letters to form the
surprise answer, as suggested by the above
cartoon.

Print
answer
here " ⎕⎕ " ⎕⎕⎕ ⎕⎕⎕⎕⎕⎕

JUMBLE

Unscramble these four Jumbles, one letter to each square, to form four ordinary words.

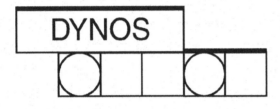

DYNOS

SABIN

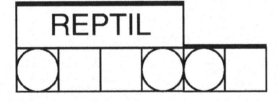

REPTIL

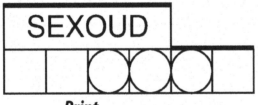

SEXOUD

I understand he was fat before he started gambling

He never wins

WHAT HE DID AT THE LONDON CASINO.

Now arrange the circled letters to form the surprise answer, as suggested by the above cartoon.

Print answer here

"   "

JUMBLE

Unscramble these four Jumbles, one letter to each square, to form four ordinary words.

SILLE

DENEY

AGOVEY

MALFEE

Give me a
hand, buddy

Sure,
pal

THE CARPENTERS
WORKED WELL
TOGETHER
BECAUSE THEY
WERE----

Now arrange the circled letters to form the surprise answer, as suggested by the above cartoon.

Print
answer
here

◯◯ THE ◯◯◯◯ " ◯◯◯◯◯ "

93

JUMBLE®

Unscramble these four Jumbles, one letter to each square, to form four ordinary words.

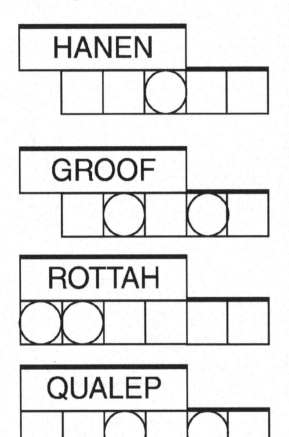

HANEN

GROOF

ROTTAH

QUALEP

WHAT THE NEIGH-
BORS LIKED TO
DO ON LAUNDRY
DAY.

Now arrange the circled letters to form the surprise answer, as suggested by the above cartoon.

Print answer here " ⬡⬡⬡⬡⬡ " ⬡⬡⬡

JUMBLE®

Unscramble these four Jumbles, one letter to each square, to form four ordinary words.

TANBO

VUEMA

WUTTIO

LUPCOE

It'll be fine in no time

Are you sure? It looks dead to me

WHEN THE TREE DOCTOR PROMISED TO SAVE THE OAK HE----

Now arrange the circled letters to form the surprise answer, as suggested by the above cartoon.

Print answer here

ON A

JUMBLE®

Unscramble these four Jumbles, one letter to each square, to form four ordinary words.

ROBAR

ALTNA

AGCUTH

BLITAR

Not exactly gourmet, but filling

A POPULAR WAY
TO GRAB A
FAST LUNCH.

Now arrange the circled letters to form the surprise answer, as suggested by the above cartoon.

Print answer here ◯ ◯◯ " ◯◯◯◯ "

JUMBLE®

Unscramble these four Jumbles, one letter to each square, to form four ordinary words.

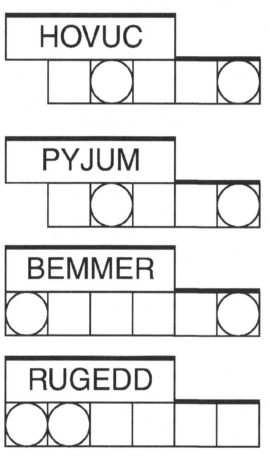

HOVUC

PYJUM

BEMMER

RUGEDD

Have one. It'll loosen you up

I'm drunk on sobriety

THE TEETOTALER WAS KNOWN FOR HIS----

Now arrange the circled letters to form the surprise answer, as suggested by the above cartoon.

Print answer here " "

JUMBLE®

Unscramble these four Jumbles, one letter to each square, to form four ordinary words.

TELAH

CLUNE

PECILS

VESSUR

Welcome to my home

"#$%_& welcome. %&*!! awwk.

WHEN HIS PARROT GREETED THEM WITH FOUL LANGUAGE, THEY WERE---

Now arrange the circled letters to form the surprise answer, as suggested by the above cartoon.

Print answer here

JUMBLE®

Unscramble these four Jumbles, one letter to each square, to form four ordinary words.

SNAIE

LEVAT

FUSULE

MINKOO

... and then there was the time I fell asleep on the bench

He's good

THE POPULAR AFTER-DINNER SPEAKER TALKED ABOUT----

Now arrange the circled letters to form the surprise answer, as suggested by the above cartoon.

Print answer here

Unscramble these four Jumbles, one letter
to each square, to form four ordinary words.

UPOHC

BLAYK

CHAWES

RAHDLE

They're attacking.
Let's get them

WHEN THE SOL-
DIERS HAD A
SNOWBALL FIGHT,
IT TURNED
INTO A---

Now arrange the circled letters to form the
surprise answer, as suggested by the above
cartoon.

Print answer here

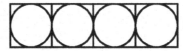

JUMBLE

Unscramble these four Jumbles, one letter
to each square, to form four ordinary words.

STEUG

CHABT

NUCCOR

ZIGHAN

THE VIOLINIST
VISITED THE
DOCTOR BECAUSE
HE WAS---

Now arrange the circled letters to form the
surprise answer, as suggested by the above
cartoon.

Print "◯◯◯◯-◯◯◯◯◯◯◯"
answer
here

JUMBLE®

Unscramble these four Jumbles, one letter to each square, to form four ordinary words.

NOFEL

TIPAL

RUBBGY

PRACET

For you, Mrs. Fligger

You're late. Sit down

WHAT HE BROUGHT THE MEAN OLD TEACHER.

Now arrange the circled letters to form the surprise answer, as suggested by the above cartoon.

Print answer here   A   " ◯◯◯◯ " ◯◯◯◯◯

JUMBLE®

Unscramble these four Jumbles, one letter to each square, to form four ordinary words.

OPTIV

ZIRPE

DIOING

REDUSS

You're the best, Sam

Here's to you

A ROUND ON THE HOUSE LEFT THE CUSTOMERS IN---

Now arrange the circled letters to form the surprise answer, as suggested by the above cartoon.

Print answer here

" "

JUMBLE®

Unscramble these four Jumbles, one letter
to each square, to form four ordinary words.

ATING

HOCEK

HIRTED

MUJERP

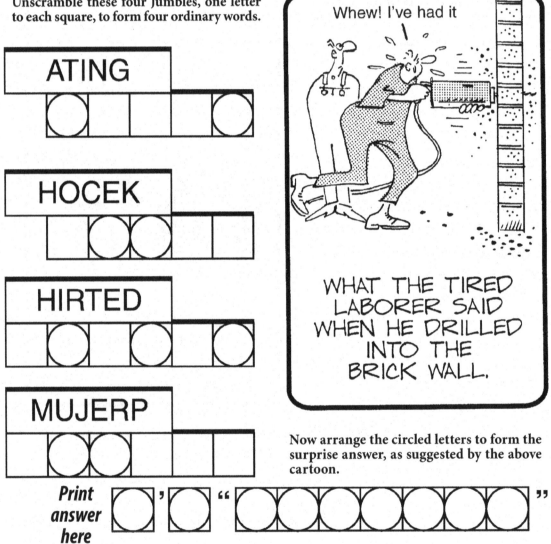

Whew! I've had it

WHAT THE TIRED
LABORER SAID
WHEN HE DRILLED
INTO THE
BRICK WALL.

Now arrange the circled letters to form the
surprise answer, as suggested by the above
cartoon.

*Print
answer
here* ☐'☐ " ☐☐☐☐☐☐☐ "

JUMBLE

Unscramble these four Jumbles, one letter
to each square, to form four ordinary words.

NISHY

RETEB

NIANIZ

TAPECK

You're late.
You're grounded

But it's
Saturday
night

THE LAST THING
A TEENAGER
WANTS TO BE.

Now arrange the circled letters to form the
surprise answer, as suggested by the above
cartoon.

Print answer here

JUMBLE®

Unscramble these four Jumbles, one letter to each square, to form four ordinary words.

MARFE

SHECS

LABERV

MINDOO

I reduced our debt by 2 million drachmas

WHAT THE KING REDUCED WHEN HE SOLD THE ROYAL CROWNS.

Now arrange the circled letters to form the surprise answer, as suggested by the above cartoon.

Print answer here HIS " ◯◯◯◯ ◯◯◯◯ "

JUMBLE®

Unscramble these four Jumbles, one letter
to each square, to form four ordinary words.

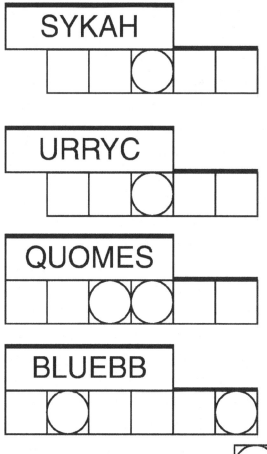

SYKAH

URRYC

QUOMES

BLUEBB

Clean this mess
to the
four walls

A TEEN'S ROOM
IS OFTEN IN
THIS SHAPE.

Now arrange the circled letters to form the
surprise answer, as suggested by the above
cartoon.

Print answer here

JUMBLE®

Unscramble these four Jumbles, one letter
to each square, to form four ordinary words.

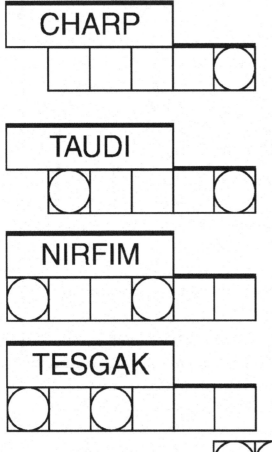

CHARP

TAUDI

NIRFIM

TESGAK

There he is.
He's limping

Must've
turned
his ankle

WHAT THE COPS
USED TO CATCH
THE FENCE.

Now arrange the circled letters to form the
surprise answer, as suggested by the above
cartoon.

Print answer here ⬡⬡⬡ " ⬡⬡⬡⬡ "

JUMBLE

Unscramble these four Jumbles, one letter to each square, to form four ordinary words.

BLYUL

CYDEA

CRYLEE

KLARET

I can send and receive all messages

I'll deliver this immediately

WHEN THE TELE-GRAPH OFFICE WAS COMPLETED, THE OPERATOR DECLARED IT---

Now arrange the circled letters to form the surprise answer, as suggested by the above cartoon.

Print answer here " ⬡⬡⬡⬡⬡ " – ⬡⬡⬡⬡⬡⬡

JUMBLE®

Unscramble these four Jumbles, one letter to each square, to form four ordinary words.

TULFE

ERQUE

RYMILG

KENASH

... and here are your winnings

WHERE A PRO GOLFER WHO HITS THE GREENS IS LIKELY TO END UP.

Now arrange the circled letters to form the surprise answer, as suggested by the above cartoon.

Print answer here IN "   "

110

JUMBLE®

Unscramble these four Jumbles, one letter to each square, to form four ordinary words.

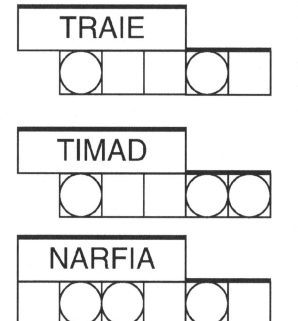

TRAIE

TIMAD

NARFIA

SPENOR

I can hardly straighten up

WHAT THE RIDER SUFFERED AFTER THE CROSS-COUNTRY RAIL TRIP.

Now arrange the circled letters to form the surprise answer, as suggested by the above cartoon.

Print answer here

JUMBLE®

Unscramble these four Jumbles, one letter to each square, to form four ordinary words.

DEFAM

KELLN

MARFFI

NALTED

Let's have lunch

I've got to finish this dough

WHEN HE VISITED HIS PAL THE BAKER, INDEED HE FOUND A----

Now arrange the circled letters to form the surprise answer, as suggested by the above cartoon.

Print answer here

IN " "

JUMBLE®

Unscramble these four Jumbles, one letter to each square, to form four ordinary words.

GULEN

CENUD

BOUSTE

BOFRID

I can't get them to move

It's sure hot

YOU MIGHT SAY THAT LYING IN THE SHADE TURNED THE STEER INTO THIS.

Now arrange the circled letters to form the surprise answer, as suggested by the above cartoon.

Print answer here "⬭⬭⬭⬭⬭⬭" ⬭⬭⬭⬭

JUMBLE®

Unscramble these four Jumbles, one letter to each square, to form four ordinary words.

POUMI

ORNOH

PHUDEL

NARTTY

What a handsome couple. Let me make you my special drink

WHAT THE POLI-
TICIAN DID
WHEN HE HOSTED
THE FUND-RAISER.

Now arrange the circled letters to form the surprise answer, as suggested by the above cartoon.

Print answer here " ⬡⬡⬡⬡⬡⬡ " IT ⬡⬡

JUMBLE®

Unscramble these four Jumbles, one letter to each square, to form four ordinary words.

FETHY

OPYPP

MIDOWS

FLOBIE

I have all my outfits made

A WELL-DRESSED MAN WITH SCUFFED SHOES LACKS THIS.

Now arrange the circled letters to form the surprise answer, as suggested by the above cartoon.

Print answer here " ◯◯◯◯◯◯ "

JUMBLE®

Unscramble these four Jumbles, one letter to each square, to form four ordinary words.

FEASH

CHELE

HODISM

WADROC

... and the juice of two limes

Mmmm, this is wonderful

WHAT THE BARTEN-DER SAID WHEN HE SHARED HIS EXOTIC DRINK RECIPE.

Now arrange the circled letters to form the surprise answer, as suggested by the above cartoon.

Print answer here " ◯◯◯◯ ' ◯ ◯◯◯ "

JUMBLE

Unscramble these four Jumbles, one letter
to each square, to form four ordinary words.

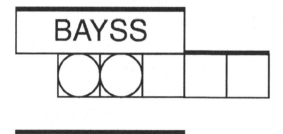
BAYSS

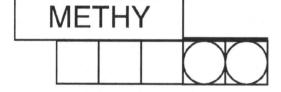
METHY

SYTRUT

AROTTE

Any
gas?

Come
aboard

WHEN THE YACHT
RAN OUT OF FUEL,
EVERYBODY ENDED
UP IN----

Now arrange the circled letters to form the
surprise answer, as suggested by the above
cartoon.

Print
answer THE
here

JUMBLE®

Unscramble these four Jumbles, one letter
to each square, to form four ordinary words.

VOBEA

UPYTT

MYSAID

MIRBLE

You will now
begin your
deliberations

WHAT THE DEFENSE
DID WHEN THE
JUDGE ADDRESSED
THE JURY.

Now arrange the circled letters to form the
surprise answer, as suggested by the above
cartoon.

Print answer here

JUMBLE®

Unscramble these four Jumbles, one letter
to each square, to form four ordinary words.

EGGAU

VARBE

LEPPUR

EEFELC

Let me
try the
blush

It's expensive
but worth it

A GOOD WAY
TO BUY
COSMETICS.

Now arrange the circled letters to form the
surprise answer, as suggested by the above
cartoon.

Print
answer AT " 〇〇〇〇 " 〇〇〇〇〇
here

JUMBLE®

Unscramble these four Jumbles, one letter
to each square, to form four ordinary words.

TUMON

MOPET

BETASK

PORTHY

For 40 years of loyal
service here's to...

What a
nice
gesture

WHEN EVERYBODY
STOOD FOR THE
TOAST, IT WAS——

Now arrange the circled letters to form the
surprise answer, as suggested by the above
cartoon.

Print answer here " ＿＿＿＿＿＿＿ " ＿＿

JUMBLE®

Unscramble these four Jumbles, one letter to each square, to form four ordinary words.

YLSYH

CONTH

RAPHEC

LEMING

The teachings of Darwin

...and Socrates

Hey, you guys — knock it off

WHEN THE SCHOLARS TOOK A NIGHT FLIGHT, THEIR CONVERSATION WAS ON A----

Now arrange the circled letters to form the surprise answer, as suggested by the above cartoon.

Print answer here

◯◯◯◯ " ◯◯◯◯◯ "

JUMBLE®

Unscramble these four Jumbles, one letter to each square, to form four ordinary words.

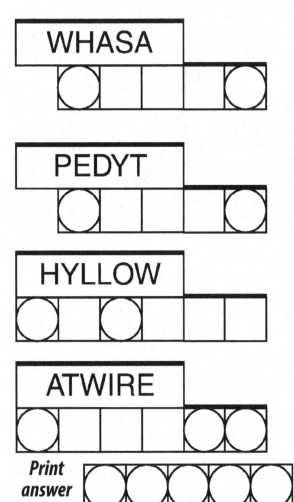

WHASA

PEDYT

HYLLOW

ATWIRE

Look at those breakers

It's about time

WHEN THE SURFERS SAW THE BIG WAVES, THEY SAID IT WAS---

Now arrange the circled letters to form the surprise answer, as suggested by the above cartoon.

Print answer here

THE " "

JUMBLE

Unscramble these four Jumbles, one letter to each square, to form four ordinary words.

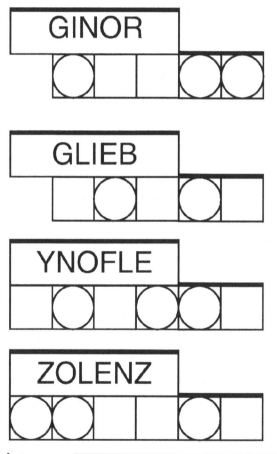

GINOR

GLIEB

YNOFLE

ZOLENZ

Mom, you've got e-mail

HOW SHE FINISHED THE LAUNDRY WHEN THE DRYER BROKE.

Now arrange the circled letters to form the surprise answer, as suggested by the above cartoon.

Print answer here BY

123

JUMBLE®

Unscramble these four Jumbles, one letter
to each square, to form four ordinary words.

CERDY

DUMON

CENNAD

ABBOOM

I'll take it

$50,000

WHAT THE FIRE-
MAN INHERITED
FROM HIS
RICH UNCLE.

Now arrange the circled letters to form the
surprise answer, as suggested by the above
cartoon.

Print
answer
here

TO

JUMBLE®

Unscramble these four Jumbles, one letter
to each square, to form four ordinary words.

KAFLE

TACCH

DOPAME

HALVIS

That Mr. Van Snoot got
in again without paying

THE MISER
SNEAKED INTO THE
ICE RINK BECAUSE
HE WAS----

Now arrange the circled letters to form the
surprise answer, as suggested by the above
cartoon.

*Print
answer
here* A

125

JUMBLE®

Unscramble these four Jumbles, one letter to each square, to form four ordinary words.

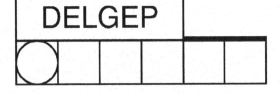

RUETT

CANKK

DELGEP

GARUJA

And Leslie can be not so nice

Did you hear what Jill did?

HOW SOME SCHOOL-GIRLS PICK THEIR FRIENDS.

Now arrange the circled letters to form the surprise answer, as suggested by the above cartoon.

Print answer here

JUMBLE®

Unscramble these four Jumbles, one letter to each square, to form four ordinary words.

DAIBE

RYHUR

QUETEA

STEJAM

This pill should fix you up fine

WHAT THE COP-TURNED-PHYSICIAN DID FOR HIS PATIENT'S PAIN.

Now arrange the circled letters to form the surprise answer, as suggested by the above cartoon.

Print answer here " ⃝⃝⃝⃝⃝⃝⃝⃝ " IT

JUMBLE®

Unscramble these four Jumbles, one letter to each square, to form four ordinary words.

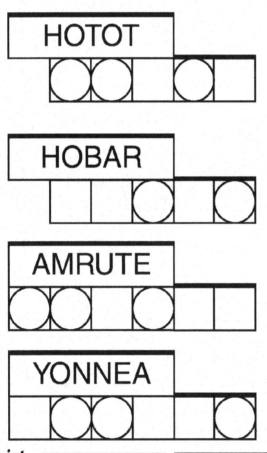

HOTOT

HOBAR

AMRUTE

YONNEA

I need a
number four

No more. It's
too complicated

He only uses
fresh ingredients

THE BUSY COOK
STOPPED USING
THE HERB RECIPE
BECAUSE HE----

Now arrange the circled letters to form the surprise answer, as suggested by the above cartoon.

Print answer here

OF

JUMBLE

Unscramble these four Jumbles, one letter
to each square, to form four ordinary words.

RAPEP

BIRAB

MORNED

TOENED

I had dinner
with my friend
Mayor Squeedunk,
then I met...

Goodness,
Hermione,
you sure
get around

WHAT SHE TURNED
INTO WHEN SHE
GOT DIVORCED.

Now arrange the circled letters to form the
surprise answer, as suggested by the above
cartoon.

Print
answer **A**
here

" "

JUMBLE®

Unscramble these four Jumbles, one letter to each square, to form four ordinary words.

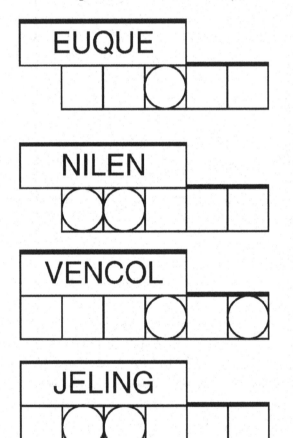

EUQUE

NILEN

VENCOL

JELING

This place is a dump

WHEN THE FIDDLER WAS SHOWN A DIRTY HOTEL ROOM, HE CALLED IT A---

Now arrange the circled letters to form the surprise answer, as suggested by the above cartoon.

Print answer here

JUMBLE®

Unscramble these four Jumbles, one letter to each square, to form four ordinary words.

MEPIR

MOBOL

RAPTYN

WOLTAL

90 minutes for a table

I'm starving

WHAT THE HEAVY-SET DINERS HAD AT THE RESTAURANT.

Now arrange the circled letters to form the surprise answer, as suggested by the above cartoon.

Print answer here A " ◯◯◯◯ " ◯◯◯◯◯◯◯◯

131

JUMBLE®

Unscramble these four Jumbles, one letter to each square, to form four ordinary words.

DABNY

PAROE

DOYLOG

RAHBOR

First, I helped this little old lady across the street, which made me miss my train. Then...

OFTEN USED TO PULL THE WOOL OVER HER EYES.

Now arrange the circled letters to form the surprise answer, as suggested by the above cartoon.

Print answer here A ⬚⬚⬚⬚ " ⬚⬚⬚⬚ "

JUMBLE®

Unscramble these four Jumbles, one letter
to each square, to form four ordinary words.

NOVEY

HEMRY

METHEL

LIVEEW

I'm so busy. I'll
be here all night

THE CLOCK MAKER
STAYED LATER
BECAUSE HE ENJOYED
WORKING ---

Now arrange the circled letters to form the
surprise answer, as suggested by the above
cartoon.

Print answer here " ⚪⚪⚪⚪ ⚪⚪⚪⚪ "

JUMBLE®

Unscramble these four Jumbles, one letter to
each square, to form four ordinary words.

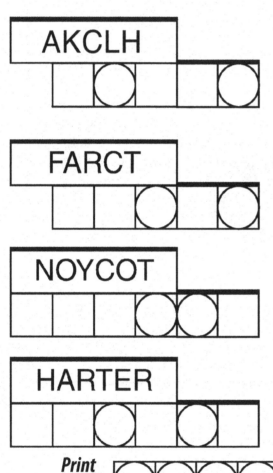

AKCLH

FARCT

NOYCOT

HARTER

Why didn't
you have it
serviced?

Sorry, folks,
I'll have it
fixed in
no time

WHAT THE LAND-
LORD DID WHEN
THE FURNACE
FAILED.

Now arrange the circled letters to form the
surprise answer, as suggested by the above
cartoon.

Print
answer
here

☐☐☐☐ THE " ☐☐☐☐ "

JUMBLE®

Unscramble these four Jumbles, one letter
to each square, to form four ordinary words.

MEWNO

SQUET

NESING

BOCIXE

That's it! No more
chocolate or
cream puffs

SHE WENT ON A
DIET BECAUSE
SHE WAS---

Now arrange the circled letters to form the
surprise answer, as suggested by the above
cartoon.

Print "⃝⃝⃝" ON ⃝⃝⃝⃝⃝⃝
answer
here

135

JUMBLE®

Unscramble these four Jumbles, one letter
to each square, to form four ordinary words.

TOSOP

ROPAN

LEMDEY

HOKOUN

First separate
whites and colors

WHAT HER
COLLEGE-BOUND
SON DID WHEN MOM
TAUGHT HIM TO
DO LAUNDRY.

Now arrange the circled letters to form the
surprise answer, as suggested by the above
cartoon.

Print answer here " ⬡⬡⬡⬡⬡⬡ " IT ⬡⬡

JUMBLE

Unscramble these four Jumbles, one letter to each square, to form four ordinary words.

REFIA

GRABE

LARIAC

FELBAF

How's the sandwich?

OK, nothing special

HOW THE DINING CRITIC DESCRIBED THE FOOD AT THE CARNIVAL.

Now arrange the circled letters to form the surprise answer, as suggested by the above cartoon.

Print answer here

JUMBLE®

Unscramble these four Jumbles, one letter to each square, to form four ordinary words.

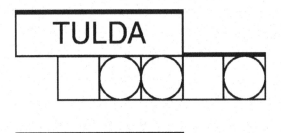

TULDA

ASTUE

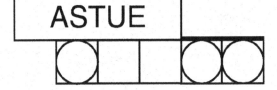

YODMEB

KENALT

She's got the look

Head up, shoulders back

WHAT IT TAKES TO LEARN TO WALK DOWN A FASHION RUNWAY.

Now arrange the circled letters to form the surprise answer, as suggested by the above cartoon.

Print answer here A " ☐☐☐☐☐ " ☐☐☐☐☐☐☐☐

JUMBLE

Unscramble these four Jumbles, one letter to each square, to form four ordinary words.

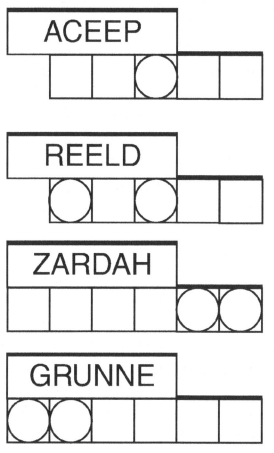

ACEEP

REELD

ZARDAH

GRUNNE

We'll see how he feels in the morning

WHEN THE PRISONER WAS HOSPITALIZED, HIS PROGNOSIS WAS---

Now arrange the circled letters to form the surprise answer, as suggested by the above cartoon.

Print answer here " ◯◯◯◯◯◯◯◯ "

JUMBLE®

Unscramble these four Jumbles, one letter
to each square, to form four ordinary words.

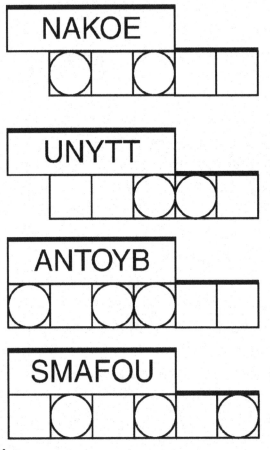

NAKOE

UNYTT

ANTOYB

SMAFOU

En garde! Try it,
Gladys, it's fun

WHAT SHE DID
WHEN SHE DATED
THE FENCING
STAR.

Now arrange the circled letters to form the
surprise answer, as suggested by the above
cartoon.

Print
answer
here

A " " IT

JUMBLE®

Unscramble these four Jumbles, one letter to each square, to form four ordinary words.

UNREP

WATHE

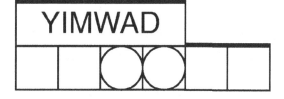

YIMWAD

HOCCUR

E-Q-U-I-O-U-S. I win!

Oh, yeah! Not so fast

WHEN THE SOLDIERS HAD A SPELLING CONTEST, IT TURNED INTO----

Now arrange the circled letters to form the surprise answer, as suggested by the above cartoon.

Print answer here A "  "

JUMBLE®

Unscramble these four Jumbles, one letter to each square, to form four ordinary words.

TREXE

BOMIL

FRILCO

CLUSKE

You can hardly walk here

They'll need lots of brooms

WHEN THE PIGEONS INVADED THE TOWN SQUARE, THEY BROUGHT A----

Now arrange the circled letters to form the surprise answer, as suggested by the above cartoon.

Print answer here

"◯◯◯◯◯" OF ◯◯◯◯◯◯◯

JUMBLE®

Unscramble these four Jumbles, one letter to each square, to form four ordinary words.

YUJIC

PULIT

NARREB

COALJE

Everybody in position.
_____ Pay close attention

THE DANCE INSTRUCTOR DEMANDED THE STUDENTS DO THIS.

Now arrange the circled letters to form the surprise answer, as suggested by the above cartoon.

Print answer here " ◯◯◯ " THE ◯◯◯◯

JUMBLE®

Unscramble these four Jumbles, one letter
to each square, to form four ordinary words.

GEEBI

YABBE

ENGLIT

GLOONB

I'd like to spend
the rest of my
life with you

Marvin, do
you mean...?

WHEN THEIR
CONVERSATION
TURNED TO MAR-
RIAGE, SHE
FOUND IT---

Now arrange the circled letters to form the
surprise answer, as suggested by the above
cartoon.

Print answer here " ⬡⬡⬡⬡⬡⬡⬡⬡ "

JUMBLE®

Unscramble these four Jumbles, one letter to each square, to form four ordinary words.

TOTID

PAPYL

WHAT THE SALES-MAN GOT WHEN HE MADE THE BIG SALE.

CADIVE

LEPOAR

Now arrange the circled letters to form the surprise answer, as suggested by the above cartoon.

Print answer here

 THE " "

JUMBLE®

Unscramble these four Jumbles, one letter to each square, to form four ordinary words.

LYGUL

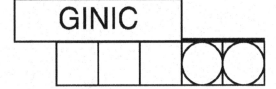

GINIC

LAMAMM

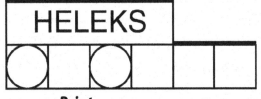

HELEKS

For you, Mrs. Swinggglebot

FINAL TEST TODAY

THE GEOMETRY STUDENT GOT A GOOD GRADE BE- CAUSE HE KNEW---

Now arrange the circled letters to form the surprise answer, as suggested by the above cartoon.

Print answer here

THE

JUMBLE®

Unscramble these four Jumbles, one letter
to each square, to form four ordinary words.

DYNAD

HORAC

JERIGG

GAMADE

WHAT THE REALTOR
DID WHEN THE
COUPLE FOUND
A HOUSE THEY
LIKED.

Now arrange the circled letters to form the
surprise answer, as suggested by the above
cartoon.

Print answer here " ◯◯◯◯◯ " ◯◯

JUMBLE®

Unscramble these four Jumbles, one letter
to each square, to form four ordinary words.

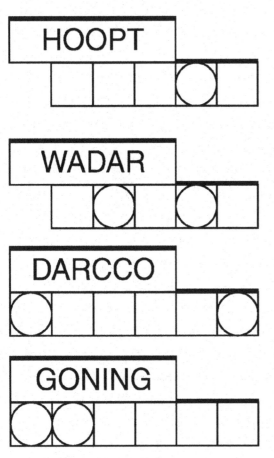

HOOPT

WADAR

DARCCO

GONING

That's lovely

It's what I love
to do

HE BECAME AN
ARTIST BECAUSE
HE FELT----

Now arrange the circled letters to form the
surprise answer, as suggested by the above
cartoon.

Print answer here " ⬡⬡⬡⬡⬡ " ⬡⬡ IT

JUMBLE®

Unscramble these four Jumbles, one letter to each square, to form four ordinary words.

NOPLY

NABAL

LIMFAY

BLOSMY

53, 54, 55, 56, 57...
One is missing

WHAT THE SHEP-
HERD DISCOVERED
WHEN HE COUNTED
HIS FLOCK.

Now arrange the circled letters to form the surprise answer, as suggested by the above cartoon.

Print answer here A ⬜⬜⬜⬜ ON THE ⬜⬜⬜

JUMBLE®

Unscramble these four Jumbles, one letter to each square, to form four ordinary words.

DULGI

CUMIS

TACTIN

NITMAR

What's taking so long?

Where's my order?

THE HOT-DOG VENDOR FIRED HIS HELPER BECAUSE HE DIDN'T----

Now arrange the circled letters to form the surprise answer, as suggested by the above cartoon.

Print answer here

☐☐☐ **THE** ☐☐☐☐☐☐☐

JUMBLE

Unscramble these four Jumbles, one letter to each square, to form four ordinary words.

ETHUC

UPMEL

HUDOLS

ZEEWEH

14 pies in
20 minutes

Where does he put them?

WHAT THE PIE-EATING CHAMP DID TO THE COMPETITION.

Now arrange the circled letters to form the surprise answer, as suggested by the above cartoon.

Print answer here

JUMBLE®

Unscramble these four Jumbles, one letter
to each square, to form four ordinary words.

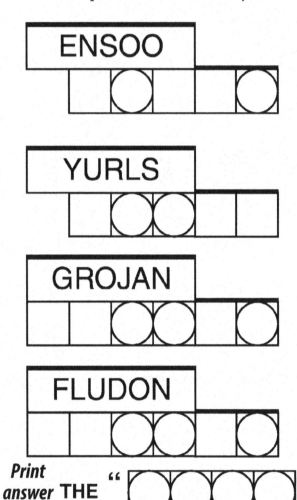

ENSOO

YURLS

GROJAN

FLUDON

UH OH, ON
YOUR LEFT

A TOURNAMENT
GOLFER TRIES
TO AVOID THIS.

Now arrange the circled letters to form the
surprise answer, as suggested by the above
cartoon.

Print
answer THE "⬡⬡⬡⬡" ⬡⬡⬡⬡⬡⬡⬡
here

JUMBLE®

Unscramble these four Jumbles, one letter to each square, to form four ordinary words.

KANET

PROWE

NIAMEA

YOTHER

You're falling behind, Ms. Vickers

Tomorrow's another day

IN
OUT

WHAT SHE ACCOMPLISHED AT HER FULL-TIME JOB.

Now arrange the circled letters to form the surprise answer, as suggested by the above cartoon.

Print answer here

JUMBLE®

Unscramble these four Jumbles, one letter
to each square, to form four ordinary words.

MONDE

HOACC

SACULE

YERSIM

Mmmm, good. Let's get a
dozen for later

TOO MANY
DOUGHNUTS MAY
NOT BE WHOLE-
SOME, BUT
THEY ARE----

Now arrange the circled letters to form the
surprise answer, as suggested by the above
cartoon.

Print answer here " ☐◯◯◯◯ - ◯◯◯◯◯ "

JUMBLE®

Unscramble these four Jumbles, one letter to each square, to form four ordinary words.

ZAUGE

UPPYP

SNODEC

URRUMM

I just love the smell of the evergreen

WHAT THE FAMILY DID TO THEIR HOME FOR THE HOLIDAYS.

Now arrange the circled letters to form the surprise answer, as suggested by the above cartoon.

Print answer here " ⬡⬡⬡⬡⬡⬡⬡ " IT ⬡⬡

JUMBLE®

Unscramble these four Jumbles, one letter to each square, to form four ordinary words.

KNACS

TOODU

OCHOLS

BLOTEG

They're dreamy

Let's not stare

GOOD LOOKS CAN ATTRACT THESE.

Now arrange the circled letters to form the surprise answer, as suggested by the above cartoon.

Print answer here

156

JUMBLE®

Unscramble these four Jumbles, one letter to each square, to form four ordinary words.

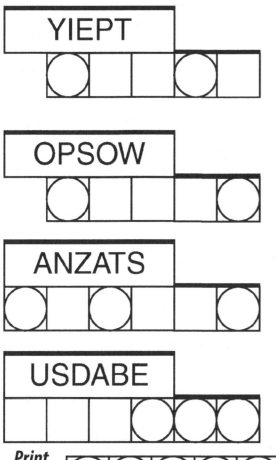

YIEPT

OPSOW

ANZATS

USDABE

This brings back memories

Remember when...?

WHEN THEY DROVE BY THEIR ALMA MATER, THEY----

Now arrange the circled letters to form the surprise answer, as suggested by the above cartoon.

Print answer here

THE

JUMBLE®

Unscramble these four Jumbles, one letter
to each square, to form four ordinary words.

NEEMY

OSKET

MANTED

SETTEA

I guess I've
put on a few
pounds

DESPITE A TIGHT
BUDGET, HE
BOUGHT A NEW
TUXEDO WHEN IT
WAS HARD TO----

Now arrange the circled letters to form the
surprise answer, as suggested by the above
cartoon.

Print
answer
here

JUMBLE®

Unscramble these four Jumbles, one letter to each square, to form four ordinary words.

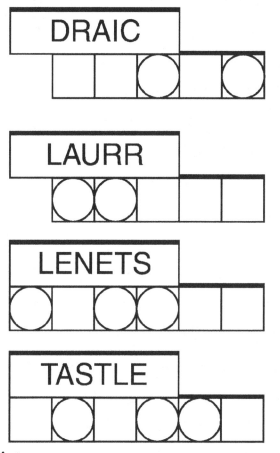

DRAIC

LAURR

LENETS

TASTLE

Nine...10...it's over

WHERE THE LOSER
ENDED UP IN THE
OUTDOOR BOXING
MATCH.

Now arrange the circled letters to form the surprise answer, as suggested by the above cartoon.

Print answer here   THE " "

JUMBLE

Unscramble these four Jumbles, one letter to each square, to form four ordinary words.

SOPIE

REMEB

INFURA

CRIMET

Just like old times

For you, sis

WITH EVERYONE HOME FOR THE HOLIDAYS, MOM AND DAD ENJOYED THEIR---

Now arrange the circled letters to form the surprise answer, as suggested by the above cartoon.

Print answer here " ◯◯◯◯◯◯◯◯ "

JUMBLE

Unscramble these four Jumbles, one letter to each square, to form four ordinary words.

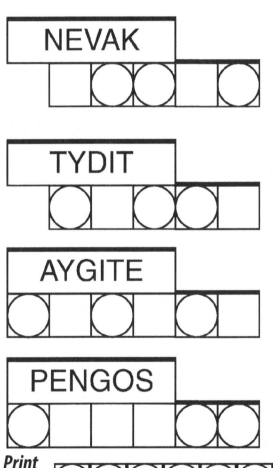

NEVAK

TYDIT

AYGITE

PENGOS

July 4, 1776
War of 1812
December 1941
etc. etc. etc.

Take your seats

Allison, how about lunch today?

WHAT THE COED CONCENTRATED ON IN HISTORY CLASS.

Now arrange the circled letters to form the surprise answer, as suggested by the above cartoon.

Print answer here

"___"

161

JUMBLE®

Unscramble these four Jumbles, one letter to each square, to form four ordinary words.

NACAL

FOOLI

YONIFT

REMPIT

Give her some air

Nice job,
Miss La Farce

THE ACTRESS GOT
THE PART BECAUSE
SHE COULD----

Now arrange the circled letters to form the surprise answer, as suggested by the above cartoon.

Print answer here

A

JUMBLE®

Unscramble these six Jumbles, one letter to each square, to form six ordinary words.

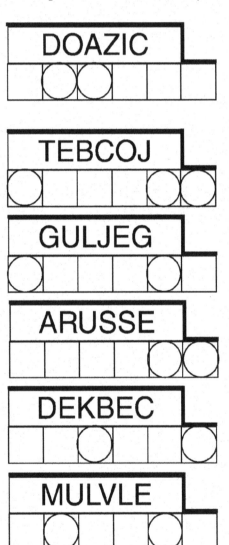

DOAZIC

TEBCOJ

GULJEG

ARUSSE

DEKBEC

MULVLE

Did you hear the one about the wildcatter's daughter?

That's it, Slick. You're through!

THE OIL RIGGER WAS FIRED BECAUSE HE----

Now arrange the circled letters to form the surprise answer, as suggested by the above cartoon.

Print answer here

A " "

164

JUMBLE®

Unscramble these six Jumbles, one letter to each square, to form six ordinary words.

GARNAH

TICUND

GICART

CATCEN

TISSAD

TERROM

ALL SALES FINAL

Cash only

No credit cards

THE PUPPETEER DIDN'T BUY THE MARIONETTES BECAUSE THERE WERE----

Now arrange the circled letters to form the surprise answer, as suggested by the above cartoon.

Print answer here

JUMBLE

Unscramble these six Jumbles, one letter to each square, to form six ordinary words.

NEXETT

SAMTIG

TRIAFY

GERELD

SILAMY

YERFIN

We can sneak down the stairs and out the back door

WHAT THE GENER-ALS PLOTTED WHEN THEIR WIVES DRAGGED THEM TO THE OPERA.

Now arrange the circled letters to form the surprise answer, as suggested by the above cartoon.

Print answer here

AN "⬡⬡⬡⬡⬡" ⬡⬡⬡⬡⬡⬡⬡⬡⬡

JUMBLE®

Unscramble these six Jumbles, one letter to each square, to form six ordinary words.

CAMIAN

LUNYUR

AREPPA

DANAGE

NAFELL

BENTON

First, I'll trim all the bushes, then I'll water and...

MAINTAINING THE FACTORY LAND-SCAPING MADE HIM THE---

Now arrange the circled letters to form the surprise answer, as suggested by the above cartoon.

Print answer here

" ⬡⬡⬡⬡⬡ " ⬡⬡⬡⬡⬡⬡⬡

JUMBLE®

Unscramble these six Jumbles, one letter to each square, to form six ordinary words.

HYDING

GANDIL

REEFIC

NOBIAL

DETUIL

GUNSLY

One minute it's sunny and the next...

I'm drenched

WHAT THE PICK-NICKERS EXPERIENCED WHEN THE UNEXPECTED STORM HIT.

Now arrange the circled letters to form the surprise answer, as suggested by the above cartoon.

Print answer here

A " ⬡⬡⬡⬡⬡⬡ " ⬡⬡⬡⬡⬡⬡

JUMBLE

Unscramble these six Jumbles, one letter to each square, to form six ordinary words.

TELMAD

COBNEK

PHORGE

URREBB

RALFOL

DITORR

...'til death do you part?

WHAT THE BRIDE AND GROOM DID WHEN THEY EXCHANGED RINGS.

Now arrange the circled letters to form the surprise answer, as suggested by the above cartoon.

Print answer here

" ◯◯◯◯◯ " ◯◯◯◯◯◯◯◯

JUMBLE®

Unscramble these six Jumbles, one letter to each square, to form six ordinary words.

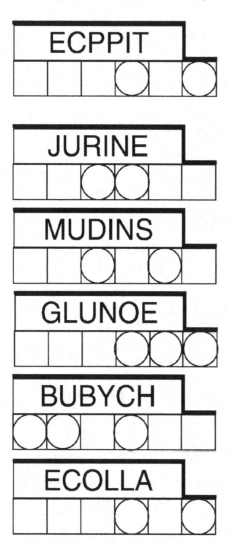

ECPPIT

JURINE

MUDINS

GLUNOE

BUBYCH

ECOLLA

You look lovely, m'lady

Never mind me. This baby's adorable

WHAT THE QUEEN DID WHEN SHE VISITED THE NURSERY.

Now arrange the circled letters to form the surprise answer, as suggested by the above cartoon.

Print answer here

THE "⬡⬡⬡⬡⬡⬡⬡"

JUMBLE

Unscramble these six Jumbles, one letter to each square, to form six ordinary words.

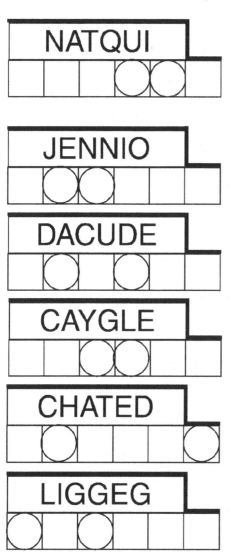

NATQUI

JENNIO

DACUDE

CAYGLE

CHATED

LIGGEG

A little to the left and lower

WHAT THE ARTIST TURNED INTO WHEN THE ART GALLERY EXHIBITED HIS WORK.

Now arrange the circled letters to form the surprise answer, as suggested by the above cartoon.

Print answer here

THE " ⬡⬡⬡⬡⬡⬡⬡ " ⬡⬡⬡⬡

JUMBLE®

Unscramble these six Jumbles, one letter to each square, to form six ordinary words.

YACENG

FESTOF

PENOLL

SLIZZE

CHIPUC

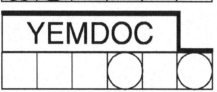

YEMDOC

That's it

Five aces... What's wrong?

HE QUIT PLAYING BECAUSE THE CARD SHARK GAVE HIM A---

Now arrange the circled letters to form the surprise answer, as suggested by the above cartoon.

Print answer here

" ◯◯◯◯◯ " ◯◯◯◯◯◯◯

JUMBLE®

Unscramble these six Jumbles, one letter
to each square, to form six ordinary words.

EIVIDD

POATIE

ENBAOM

TOPITE

DRIAFA

MIRTHE

I want to be
the best that
I can be

THE SOLDIER
TOOK EXTRA
TARGET PRACTICE
BECAUSE HE----

Now arrange the circled letters to form the
surprise answer, as suggested by the above
cartoon.

Print answer here

" ◯◯◯◯◯ " TO ◯◯◯◯◯◯◯

173

JUMBLE®

Unscramble these six Jumbles, one letter to each square, to form six ordinary words.

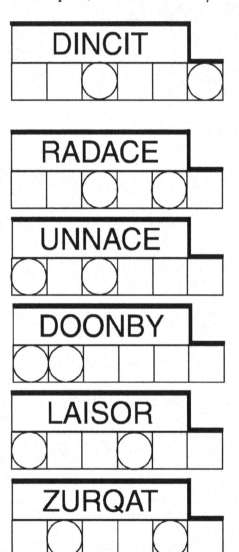

DINCIT

RADACE

UNNACE

DOONBY

LAISOR

ZURQAT

MODELS WANTED

Dolores, you'd be perfect

Not me — I'd be on my feet all day

SHE REFUSED TO BE A WARDROBE MODEL BECAUSE SHE---

Now arrange the circled letters to form the surprise answer, as suggested by the above cartoon.

Print answer here

◯◯◯◯◯◯ ' ◯ " ◯◯◯◯◯ " IT

174

JUMBLE®

Unscramble these six Jumbles, one letter to each square, to form six ordinary words.

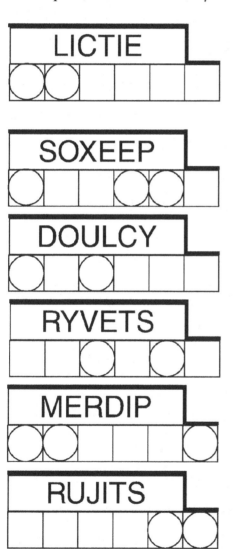

LICTIE

SOXEEP

DOULCY

RYVETS

MERDIP

RUJITS

Your resume is impressive

I bring my own vacuum

THE HOUSE CLEANER WAS HIRED BECAUSE SHE HAD A---

Now arrange the circled letters to form the surprise answer, as suggested by the above cartoon.

Print answer here

JUMBLE®

Unscramble these six Jumbles, one letter to each square, to form six ordinary words.

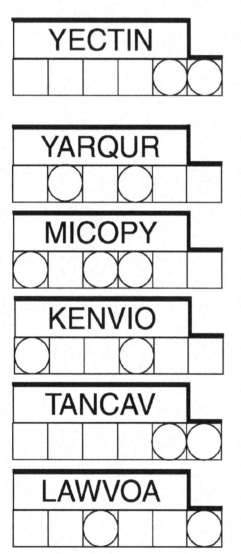

YECTIN

YARQUR

MICOPY

KENVIO

TANCAV

LAWVOA

He moves so gracefully

WHEN THE ROOSTER PRANCED AROUND THE CHICKEN COOP, IT WAS----

Now arrange the circled letters to form the surprise answer, as suggested by the above cartoon.

Print answer here

" ⬭⬭⬭⬭⬭⬭⬭ " IN ⬭⬭⬭⬭⬭⬭

JUMBLE.

Unscramble these six Jumbles, one letter
to each square, to form six ordinary words.

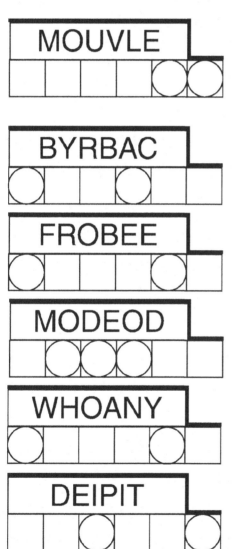

MOUVLE

BYRBAC

FROBEE

MODEOD

WHOANY

DEIPIT

Why did we
rush here?

Hurry up
and wait

SOLDIERS DO THIS
ALL THE TIME.

Now arrange the circled letters to form the
surprise answer, as suggested by the above
cartoon.

Print answer here

" ◯◯◯◯◯◯ " ◯◯◯◯◯◯◯

JUMBLE®

Unscramble these six Jumbles, one letter to each square, to form six ordinary words.

INGRYP

UTTOLE

NIPPEG

MINTIG

NATTEX

DOVNER

Better than
the others

5 5 5

WHAT THE JUDGES
CONSIDERED THE
WINNING SKATER'S
SPINS.

Now arrange the circled letters to form the surprise answer, as suggested by the above cartoon.

Print answer here

THE " ◯◯◯◯◯◯◯ " ◯◯◯◯◯

JUMBLE®

Unscramble these six Jumbles, one letter to each square, to form six ordinary words.

ENVORG

GINEEN

PREMAT

CAPMEN

HYSERR

BRONIN

How's it look?

I'm speechless!

WHAT DAD EXPERIENCED WHEN JUNIOR UNEXPECTEDLY WAXED THE CAR.

Now arrange the circled letters to form the surprise answer, as suggested by the above cartoon.

Print answer here

A " ⃝⃝⃝⃝⃝⃝⃝ " ⃝⃝⃝⃝⃝⃝

JUMBLE

Unscramble these six Jumbles, one letter
to each square, to form six ordinary words.

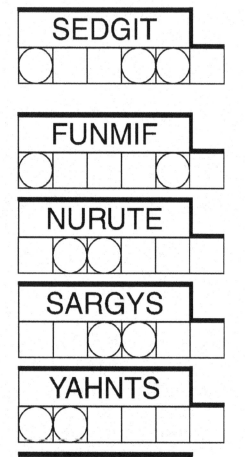

SEDGIT

FUNMIF

NURUTE

SARGYS

YAHNTS

WETSOB

Good
morning,
class

Good morning,
Mrs. Flaggersham

WHAT THE TEACHER
DISCOVERED WHEN
SHE RETURNED
FROM HER
HONEYMOON.

Now arrange the circled letters to form the
surprise answer, as suggested by the above
cartoon.

Print answer here

JUMBLE®

Unscramble these six Jumbles, one letter to each square, to form six ordinary words.

CISTEB

TICEXE

PUDETY

POSHIN

LIFRAY

YAWALY

Doc, you need to cut your overhead

THE M.D. VISITED HIS ACCOUNTANT BECAUSE IT WAS TIME FOR---

Now arrange the circled letters to form the surprise answer, as suggested by the above cartoon.

Print answer here

" ⬡⬡⬡⬡⬡⬡⬡ " ⬡⬡⬡⬡⬡⬡⬡⬡

JUMBLE®

Unscramble these six Jumbles, one letter to each square, to form six ordinary words.

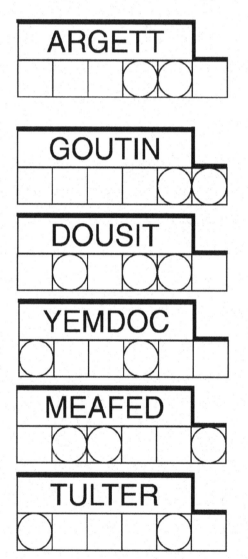

ARGETT

GOUTIN

DOUSIT

YEMDOC

MEAFED

TULTER

I hope we get there before the traffic

I'm going to hold out for a good price

WHAT THE SHEPHERD WANTED TO AVOID WHEN HE TOOK HIS FLOCK TO MARKET.

Now arrange the circled letters to form the surprise answer, as suggested by the above cartoon.

Print answer here

JUMBLE®

Unscramble these six Jumbles, one letter to each square, to form six ordinary words.

ORCEAN

LOORIE

JAVILO

BARTUN

AGMENT

UCCSAU

I'm running to the bank, dear

WHERE THE OWNER OF THE SEEDY BAR KEPT HIS MONEY.

Now arrange the circled letters to form the surprise answer, as suggested by the above cartoon.

Print answer here

IN A " ⬡⬡⬡⬡⬡ " ⬡⬡⬡⬡⬡⬡⬡

Answers

1. **Jumbles:** KNOWN GLOAT QUORUM TARGET
   Answer: What Dad said when Junior cleaned the fireplace—"GRATE WORK"

2. **Jumbles:** DOUBT ITCHY BETRAY IMPEND
   Answer: A pair of gloves can do this for a gardener—COME IN "HANDY"

3. **Jumbles:** KITTY STUNG VANISH INHALE
   Answer: What Christmas turned into when she didn't get a present—SILENT NIGHT

4. **Jumbles:** SMOKY PLAID EMBALM DAHLIA
   Answer: What he did when his manager "talked"—HE "BALKED"

5. **Jumbles:** STEED WHILE MIDWAY UNFOLD
   Answer: After working all night to solve the computer glitch it—"DAWNED" ON HIM

6. **Jumbles:** BUXOM FINIS CORNET OFFSET
   Answer: What it was worth when the movie hunk posed in a skimpy swimsuit—A "BRIEF" MENTION

7. **Jumbles:** TAKEN YODEL AROUND BAZAAR
   Answer: When the gardener won the high-stakes poker hand, he—"RAKED" IN A BUNDLE

8. **Jumbles:** PAYEE MOSSY CUPFUL DEFAME
   Answer: What the neighbors did when the smoke-belching jalopy drove by—"FUMED"

9. **Jumbles:** AGING MUSTY EXCITE BROOCH
   Answer: What the exotic dancer stripped while she drove—THE GEARS

10. **Jumbles:** HASTY STOKE BEWARE CHOSEN
    Answer: Why the astronomer went to the movie premiere—TO SEE THE STARS

11. **Jumbles:** TWINE OXIDE DECADE SHERRY
    Answer: A cold apartment can lead to this—"HEATED" WORDS

12. **Jumbles:** GORGE TUNED TURBAN MORBID
    Answer: What a prissy matron might do when told an off-color joke—TURN RED

13. **Jumbles:** CLOAK LOWLY DABBLE STURDY
    Answer: What a night watchman never does—A DAY'S WORK

14. **Jumbles:** AFTER FETID BEHAVE TREATY
    Answer: Why the drag racer took golf lessons—TO "DRIVE" BETTER

15. **Jumbles:** BOUND FACET INBORN GARISH
    Answer: What the colts liked to do—"HORSE" AROUND

16. **Jumbles:** OLDER COVEY BLEACH MARMOT
    Answer: When he took the deep-sea-diving test, he was in—OVER HIS HEAD

17. **Jumbles:** GUISE FEVER BYWORD HAGGLE
    Answer: How the carriage driver felt when he caught a cold—HOARSE AND BUGGY

18. **Jumbles:** DITTO AFOOT RECTOR SINGLE
    Answer: What Junior got when the cell phone bill arrived—A LOT OF "STATIC"

19. **Jumbles:** DOILY WRATH DEAFEN TROUGH
    Answer: A good thing to do before buying a book on trees—"LEAF" THROUGH IT

20. **Jumbles:** RAPID BRASS VANDAL LACKEY
    Answer: Where the fat lady sings at the opera—THE ARIA AREA

21. **Jumbles:** EMPTY ESSAY FLUNKY SUBWAY
    Answer: What the busy pickpocket liked to do—TAKE IT "EASY"

22. **Jumbles:** CABIN BAGGY SCURVY QUEASY
    Answer: How he described the waitress' remarks—"SAUCY"

23. **Jumbles:** PILOT CHIDE CONVOY PONDER
    Answer: When the seer's services didn't sell at the charity auction, she became—A NON-PROPHET

24. **Jumbles:** PANSY SNOWY DIVERT AROUSE
    Answer: When the tennis champ lost to the amateur, he—WAS "UPSET"

25. **Jumbles:** YOUTH PLUSH NOGGIN NEWEST
    Answer: He was a good doorman because he knew the—INS AND OUTS

26. **Jumbles:** JUROR SUITE COSTLY EXHORT
    Answer: The barber was good at this—SHORT CUTS

27. **Jumbles:** CIVIL DUCAT RELISH CAMPER
    Answer: What the butcher did for his good customer—"SLICED" THE PRICE

28. **Jumbles:** DOUGH MOUTH MUSLIN THIRTY
    Answer: This helped to pass the time when the power went out—"LIGHT" HUMOR

29. **Jumbles:** FORCE DELVE WIDEST GOLFER
    Answer: After he hung the mirror, he—"REFLECTED" ON IT

30. **Jumbles:** AWFUL NOVEL DROWSY CUDDLE
    Answer: When the artist won the poker hand, the losers said he—"DREW" WELL

31. **Jumbles:** JOLLY BASIC SQUIRM IMMUNE
    Answer: What the shoemaker listened to while he worked—"SOLE" MUSIC

32. **Jumbles:** APPLY FAUNA HYBRID JAILED
    Answer: When the bucket brigade fought the blaze, they were—ALL "FIRED" UP

33. **Jumbles:** NAÏVE SOGGY TONGUE MARVEL
    Answer: She dumped the guitarist because he wanted to—"STRING" HER ALONG

34. **Jumbles:** GAUDY MADLY ADVICE WATERY
    Answer: When the trucker passed the mountain driving test, he—MADE THE "GRADE"

35. **Jumbles:** FINAL ONION LOTION INFUSE
    Answer: What Mom faced when she ran out of window cleaner—NO "SOLUTION"

36. **Jumbles:** TACKY YEARN ZENITH SATIRE
    Answer: How the baker felt after making cakes all day—"STIR" CRAZY

37. **Jumbles:** LIVEN GAILY IMPAIR DUGOUT
    Answer: What he said when the concert was over—IT WAS "TRILLING"

38. **Jumbles:** FANCY LLAMA FIRING LAWFUL
    Answer: When she spotted a mouse in the cupboard, it was—"GNAW-FULL"

39. **Jumbles:** ACUTE BUSHY FONDLY TRUDGE
    Answer: This car is like a lengthy prison term because they're both—A LONG "STRETCH"

40. **Jumbles:** GOUGE FRUIT PENCIL IODINE
    Answer: Where she went before the high school reunion—ON A DIET

41. **Jumbles:** ODDLY ADAPT FAÇADE KINGLY
    Answer: When the executive asked the board for a company plane, his request—DIDN'T "FLY"

42. **Jumbles:** JOUST BERTH BRIDLE TEACUP
    Answer: She bought the pricey sunscreen because it was—A "SHADE" BETTER

43. **Jumbles:** WHOSE FUROR MEADOW BESTOW
    Answer: Easy to experience on a sugar-free diet—"SWEET" SORROW

44. **Jumbles:** ARRAY GROOM BIGAMY UNLIKE
    Answer: Why he quit his job on the offshore oil rig—IT WAS "BORING"

45. **Jumbles:** GLEAM BLOOD HEALTH PEWTER
    Answer: The society matrons passed up the shoe-repair offer because they were—WELL "HEELED"

46. **Jumbles:** STAID PIPER CACTUS MUSKET
    Answer: Why the young quarterback made the varsity team—HE "PASSED" THE TEST

47. **Jumbles:** GRIME WAGER CARNAL FERRET
Answer: Where the hockey player with liberal views played—AT "LEFT" WING

48. **Jumbles:** VERVE THINK GAINED DISMAL
Answer: A complex recipe can be this—HARD TO "DIGEST"

49. **Jumbles:** MAIZE BAKED FORGOT CIPHER
Answer: What the shady salesman did to the unsuspecting buyer—TOOK HIM FOR A RIDE

50. **Jumbles:** BUMPY CREEL JERSEY COUGAR
Answer: When the ring sold for a premium price, the jeweler said it was a—"GEM" OF A SALE

51. **Jumbles:** BOGUS MOTIF FRENZY BUREAU
Answer: What the jockey enjoyed—SURF AND TURF

52. **Jumbles:** DADDY GUARD GRAVEN PEPSIN
Answer: He had a hole in his sock because his wife didn't—GIVE A "DARN"

53. **Jumbles:** ENJOY AGENT BALLET WIZARD
Answer: What the teen said when his younger brother played his drums—"BEAT IT"

54. **Jumbles:** QUILT LOGIC PLENTY PARADE
Answer: How the children learned to add before computers—"DIGITALLY"

55. **Jumbles:** OFTEN SCOUR POETRY HAPPEN
Answer: When he got a boomerang for his birthday, he enjoyed many—HAPPY "RETURNS"

56. **Jumbles:** GULCH AGONY POLISH FETISH
Answer: What the instructor insisted on when the singer wanted to be a pilot—A "SOLO" FLIGHT

57. **Jumbles:** SHOWY POKER EMPIRE STICKY
Answer: What you can end up with when a candidate asks for "dough"—PIE IN THE SKY

58. **Jumbles:** LOONY TAWNY OUTCRY ROBBER
Answer: How she felt after modeling clothes all day—"WORN" OUT

59. **Jumbles:** ENSUE NOISY POPLAR HELPER
Answer: What the champion golfer offered his amateur partners—PRO'S PROSE

60. **Jumbles:** FLANK LUSTY MYSELF BURIAL
Answer: What the yachtsman found at the boat shop—A SAIL SALE

61. **Jumbles:** ADAGE GAVEL UNSOLD SUBDUE
Answer: Drinking beer while playing picnic baseball can lead to this—BASES "LOADED"

62. **Jumbles:** SLANT NAVAL LIKELY STYMIE
Answer: What Mom made when the first-grader came home from class—"SMALL" TALK

63. **Jumbles:** DIRTY JETTY ROSARY FUMBLE
Answer: What the valedictorian wore to her interview for college—A "SMART" OUTFIT

64. **Jumbles:** SIXTY DICED COMMON JANGLE
Answer: When Dad didn't help with the carpet cleaning, Mom was—"STEAMING"

65. **Jumbles:** LAUGH JUICE ELIXIR TINKLE
Answer: What the couple did when the upstairs neighbors had a dance party—"HIT" THE CEILING

66. **Jumbles:** WHOOP NEWLY ISLAND BABOON
Answer: When the tornado hunters spotted the twister, they were—"BLOWN" AWAY

67. **Jumbles:** VENOM MINER ARMADA FAUCET
Answer: What the doctor established when he mounted a diagram of the brain—A "FRAME" OF MIND

68. **Jumbles:** CRAWL AXIOM NEPHEW BEYOND
Answer: When he took too many lunches, he became—"EXPANDABLE"

69. **Jumbles:** FEINT COLIC MASCOT HANSOM
Answer: What the law professor faced when the students protested—A "CLASS" ACTION

70. **Jumbles:** ANNUL GOURD KETTLE COBALT
Answer: The banker hired the seer because he needed—A "TELLER"

71. **Jumbles:** CROUP BLOAT FEUDAL SURETY
Answer: What the florist faced when business improved—A "ROSY" FUTURE

72. **Jumbles:** VAPOR CRANK BUCKET IMPOSE
Answer: When clouds formed over the open-air theater the actor said—IT'S OVER "CAST"

73. **Jumbles:** TRULY RANCH BOUNTY BENIGN
Answer: What the cops demanded from the arson suspect—THE "BURNING" TRUTH

74. **Jumbles:** FRIAR NIPPY JOSTLE ATTAIN
Answer: When Gramps paid to fill his tires with air, he considered it—"INFLATION"

75. **Jumbles:** JOINT OBESE CHORUS BALSAM
Answer: Where the conductor placed the officers in the military orchestra—THE "BRASS" SECTION

76. **Jumbles:** MIDGE QUAKE BARROW POTTER
Answer: Tough to do after a workout—GET THE WORK OUT

77. **Jumbles:** KHAKI BANJO BUSILY SEXTON
Answer: What the golfer exclaimed when he kept hitting the ball in the water—IT'S A LINKS JINX

78. **Jumbles:** BRAND JADED BANANA SURTAX
Answer: The musicians didn't use the rickety platform because it was—A "BANNED" STAND

79. **Jumbles:** SWOON PERKY SEPTIC JACKAL
Answer: When she was "taken" by her friend's beau, she was reminded that he—WAS "TAKEN"

80. **Jumbles:** BOOTY NIECE PARODY VACUUM
Answer: What he realized when she declined the kiss at midnight—THE "DATE" WAS OVER

81. **Jumbles:** DRAWL ABATE SUBMIT KERNEL
Answer: When the analyst's forecast fell short, the investor realized it was—A "BULL" MARKET

82. **Jumbles:** GLAND TWILL CHISEL BUTLER
Answer: How the reporter got the scoop at the soup kitchen—WITH A LADLE

83. **Jumbles:** MANLY PIANO NEARBY GYPSUM
Answer: How the bowler paid for the acupuncture treatment—WITH "PIN" MONEY

84. **Jumbles:** GRIEF HOIST THRIVE DISARM
Answer: What the tennis fans said when he aced the obnoxious favorite—"SERVES" HIM RIGHT

85. **Jumbles:** PHONY WEDGE BRANDY ABOUND
Answer: The cowboy didn't join his pals in the saloon because he was—ON THE "WAGON"

86. **Jumbles:** SQUAB CROON ORIGIN GIBLET
Answer: What the king said when the storm ruined his picnic plans—THE RAIN REIGNS

87. **Jumbles:** GLORY FLOOD AUBURN CALMLY
Answer: Why the knitting group invited the storyteller—FOR A GOOD "YARN"

88. **Jumbles:** BELLE DUMPY UPKEEP STUPID
Answer: What he did when the ceiling light failed—"STEPPED" UP

89. **Jumbles:** PECAN GAMUT ALIGHT POPLIN
Answer: When the recruit was assigned a top bunk, he was—"UP" ALL NIGHT

90. **Jumbles:** SYNOD BASIN TRIPLE EXODUS
Answer: What he did at the London casino—LOST "POUNDS"

91. **Jumbles:** LISLE NEEDY VOYAGE FEMALE
Answer: The carpenters worked well together because they were—ON THE SAME "LEVEL"

92. **Jumbles:** HENNA FORGO THROAT PLAQUE
Answer: What the neighbors liked to do on laundry day—"HANG" OUT

93. **Jumbles:** BATON MAUVE OUTWIT COUPLE
Answer: When the tree doctor promised to save the oak he—WENT OUT ON A LIMB

94. **Jumbles:** ARBOR NATAL CAUGHT TRIBAL
Answer: A popular way to grab a fast lunch—A LA "CART"

95. **Jumbles:** VOUCH JUMPY MEMBER DRUDGE
Answer: The teetotaler was known for his—"DRY" HUMOR

96. **Jumbles:** LATHE UNCLE SPLICE VERSUS
Answer: When his parrot greeted them with foul language, they were—SPEECHLESS

97. **Jumbles:** ANISE VALET USEFUL KIMONO
Answer: The popular after-dinner speaker talked about—FIVE MINUTES

98. **Jumbles:** POUCH BALKY CASHEW HERALD
Answer: When the soldiers had a snowball fight, it turned into a—COLD WAR

99. **Jumbles:** GUEST BATCH CONCUR HAZING
Answer: The violinist visited the doctor because he was—HIGH-STRUNG

100. **Jumbles:** FELON PLAIT GRUBBY CARPET
Answer: What he brought the mean old teacher—A "CRAB" APPLE

101. **Jumbles:** PIVOT PRIZE INDIGO DURESS
Answer: A round on the house left the customers in—GOOD "SPIRITS"

102. **Jumbles:** GIANT CHOKE DITHER JUMPER
Answer: What the tired laborer said when he drilled into the brick wall—I'M "THROUGH"

103. **Jumbles:** SHINY BERET ZINNIA PACKET
Answer: The last thing a teenager wants to be—NINETEEN

104. **Jumbles:** FRAME CHESS VERBAL DOMINO
Answer: What the king reduced when he sold the royal crowns—HIS "OVER HEAD"

105. **Jumbles:** SHAKY CURRY MOSQUE BUBBLE
Answer: A teen's room is often in this shape—SQUARE

106. **Jumbles:** PARCH AUDIT INFIRM GASKET
Answer: What the cops used to catch the fence—HIS "GAIT"

107. **Jumbles:** BULLY DECAY CELERY TALKER
Answer: When the telegraph office was completed, the operator declared it—"CABLE"-READY

108. **Jumbles:** FLUTE QUEER GRIMLY SHAKEN
Answer: Where a pro golfer who hits the greens is likely to end up—IN THE "GREEN"

109. **Jumbles:** IRATE ADMIT FARINA PERSON
Answer: What the rider suffered after the cross-country rail trip—TRAIN STRAIN

110. **Jumbles:** FAMED KNELL AFFIRM DENTAL
Answer: When he visited his pal the baker, indeed he found a—FRIEND IN "KNEAD"

111. **Jumbles:** LUNGE DUNCE OBTUSE FORBID
Answer: You might say that lying in the shade turned the steer into this—"GROUND" BEEF

112. **Jumbles:** OPIUM HONOR UPHELD TYRANT
Answer: What the politician did when he hosted the fund-raiser—"POURED" IT ON

113. **Jumbles:** HEFTY POPPY WISDOM FOIBLE
Answer: A well-dressed man with scuffed shoes lacks this—"POLISH"

114. **Jumbles:** SHEAF LEECH MODISH COWARD
Answer: What the bartender said when he shared his exotic drink recipe—"HERE'S HOW"

115. **Jumbles:** ABYSS THYME TRUSTY ROTATE
Answer: When the yacht ran out of fuel, everybody ended up in—THE SAME BOAT

116. **Jumbles:** ABOVE PUTTY DISMAY LIMBER
Answer: What the defense did when the judge addressed the jury—RESTED

117. **Jumbles:** GAUGE BRAVE PURPLE FLEECE
Answer: A good way to buy cosmetics—AT "FACE" VALUE

118. **Jumbles:** MOUNT TEMPO BASKET TROPHY
Answer: When everybody stood for the toast, it was—"BOTTOMS" UP

119. **Jumbles:** SHYLY NOTCH PREACH MINGLE
Answer: When the scholars took a night flight, their conversation was on a—HIGH "PLANE"

120. **Jumbles:** AWASH TYPED WHOLLY WAITER
Answer: When the surfers saw the big waves, they said it was—WORTH THE "WADE"

121. **Jumbles:** GROIN BILGE FELONY NOZZLE
Answer: How she finished the laundry when the dryer broke—BY GOING ON LINE

122. **Jumbles:** DECRY MOUND CANNED BAMBOO
Answer: What the fireman inherited from his rich uncle—MONEY TO BURN

123. **Jumbles:** FLAKE CATCH POMADE LAVISH
Answer: The miser sneaked into the ice rink because he was—A CHEAP SKATE

124. **Jumbles:** UTTER KNACK PLEDGE JAGUAR
Answer: How some schoolgirls pick their friends—APART

125. **Jumbles:** ABIDE HURRY EQUATE JETSAM
Answer: What the cop-turned-physician did for his patient's pain—"ARRESTED" IT

126. **Jumbles:** TOOTH ABHOR MATURE ANYONE
Answer: The busy cook stopped using the herb recipe because he—RAN OUT OF THYME

127. **Jumbles:** PAPER RABBI MODERN DENOTE
Answer: What she turned into when she got divorced—A NAME "DROPPER"

128. **Jumbles:** QUEUE LINEN CLOVEN JINGLE
Answer: When the fiddler was shown a dirty hotel room, he called it a—VILE INN

129. **Jumbles:** PRIME BLOOM PANTRY TALLOW
Answer: What the heavyset diners had at the restaurant—A "WAIT" PROBLEM

130. **Jumbles:** BANDY OPERA GOODLY HARBOR
Answer: Often used to pull the wool over her eyes—A GOOD "YARN"

131. **Jumbles:** ENVOY RHYME HELMET WEEVIL
Answer: The clock maker stayed later because he enjoyed working—"OVER TIME"

132. **Jumbles:** CHALK CRAFT TYCOON RATHER
Answer: What the landlord did when the furnace failed—TOOK THE "HEAT"

133. **Jumbles:** WOMEN QUEST ENSIGN ICEBOX
Answer: She went on a diet because she was—"BIG" ON SWEETS

134. **Jumbles:** STOOP APRON MEDLEY UNHOOK
Answer: What her college-bound son did when Mom taught him to do laundry—"SOAKED" IT UP

135. **Jumbles:** AFIRE BARGE RACIAL BAFFLE
Answer: How the dining critic described the food at the carnival—FAIR FAIR FARE

136. **Jumbles:** ADULT SAUTE EMBODY ANKLET
Answer: What it takes to learn to walk down a fashion runway—A "MODEL" STUDENT

137. **Jumbles:** PEACE ELDER HAZARD GUNNER
Answer: When the prisoner was hospitalized, his prognosis was—"GUARDED"

138. **Jumbles:** OAKEN NUTTY BOTANY FAMOUS
Answer: What she did when she dated the fencing star—TOOK A "STAB" AT IT

139. **Jumbles:** PRUNE WHEAT MIDWAY CROUCH
Answer: When the soldiers had a spelling contest, it turned into—A "WORD" WAR

140. **Jumbles:** EXERT LIMBO FROLIC SUCKLE
Answer: When the pigeons invaded the town square, they brought a—"FLOCK" OF TROUBLE

141. **Jumbles:** JUICY TULIP BARREN CAJOLE
Answer: The dance instructor demanded the students do this—"TOE" THE LINE

142. **Jumbles:** BEIGE ABBEY TINGLE OBLONG
Answer: When their conversation turned to marriage, she found it—"ENGAGING"

143. **Jumbles:** DITTO APPLY ADVICE PAROLE
Answer: What the salesman got when he made the big sale—ALL THE "CREDIT"

144. **Jumbles:** GULLY ICING MAMMAL SHEKEL
Answer: The geometry student got a good grade because he knew—ALL THE ANGLES

145. **Jumbles:** DANDY ROACH JIGGER DAMAGE
Answer: What the realtor did when the couple found a house they liked—"HOMED" IN

146. **Jumbles:** PHOTO AWARD ACCORD NOGGIN
Answer: He became an artist because he felt—"DRAWN" TO IT

147. **Jumbles:** PYLON BANAL FAMILY SYMBOL
Answer: What the shepherd discovered when he counted his flock—A LAMB ON THE LAM

148. **Jumbles:** GUILD MUSIC INTACT MARTIN
Answer: The hot-dog vendor fired his helper because he didn't—CUT THE MUSTARD

149. **Jumbles:** CHUTE PLUME SHOULD WHEEZE
Answer: What the pie-eating champ did to the competition—CHEWED THEM UP

150. **Jumbles:** NOOSE SURLY JARGON UNFOLD
Answer: A tournament golfer tries to avoid this—THE "FORE" GROUND

151. **Jumbles:** TAKEN POWER ANEMIA THEORY
Answer: What she accomplished at her full-time job—PART-TIME WORK

152. **Jumbles:** DEMON COACH CLAUSE MISERY
Answer: Too many doughnuts may not be wholesome, but they are—"HOLE-SOME"

153. **Jumbles:** GAUZE PUPPY SECOND MURMUR
Answer: What the family did to their home for the holidays—"SPRUCED" IT UP

154. **Jumbles:** SNACK OUTDO SCHOOL GOBLET
Answer: Good looks can attract these—GOOD LOOKS

155. **Jumbles:** PIETY SWOOP STANZA ABUSED
Answer: When they drove by their alma mater, they—PASSED THE PAST

156. **Jumbles:** ENEMY STOKE TANDEM ESTATE
Answer: Despite a tight budget, he bought a new tuxedo when it was hard to—MAKE ENDS MEET

157. **Jumbles:** ACRID RURAL NESTLE LATEST
Answer: Where the loser ended up in the outdoor boxing match—UNDER THE "STARS"

158. **Jumbles:** POISE EMBER UNFAIR METRIC
Answer: With everyone home for the holidays, Mom and Dad enjoyed their—"PRESENCE"

159. **Jumbles:** KNAVE DITTY GAIETY SPONGE
Answer: What the coed concentrated on in history class—GETTING "DATES"

160. **Jumbles:** CANAL FOLIO NOTIFY PERMIT
Answer: The actress got the part because she could—FEINT A FAINT

161. **Jumbles:** ZODIAC OBJECT JUGGLE ASSURE BEDECK VELLUM
Answer: The oil rigger was fired because he—TOLD A "CRUDE" JOKE

162. **Jumbles:** HANGAR INDUCT TRAGIC ACCENT SADIST TREMOR
Answer: The puppeteer didn't buy the marionettes because there were—STRINGS ATTACHED

163. **Jumbles:** EXTENT STIGMA RATIFY LEDGER MISLAY FINERY
Answer: What the generals plotted when their wives dragged them to the opera—AN "EXIT" STRATEGY

164. **Jumbles:** MANIAC UNRULY APPEAR AGENDA FALLEN BONNET
Answer: Maintaining the factory landscaping made him the—"PLANT" MANAGER

165. **Jumbles:** DINGHY LADING FIERCE ALBINO DILUTE SNUGLY
Answer: What the picnickers experienced when the unexpected storm hit—A "SODDEN" CHANGE

166. **Jumbles:** MALTED BECKON GOPHER RUBBER FLORAL TORRID
Answer: What the bride and groom did when they exchanged rings—"BANDED" TOGETHER

167. **Jumbles:** PEPTIC INJURE NUDISM LOUNGE CHUBBY LOCALE
Answer: What the queen did when she visited the nursery—CHANGED THE "SUBJECT"

168. **Jumbles:** QUAINT ENJOIN ADDUCE LEGACY DETACH GIGGLE
Answer: What the artist turned into when the art gallery exhibited his work—THE "HANGING" JUDGE

169. **Jumbles:** AGENCY OFFSET POLLEN SIZZLE HICCUP COMEDY
Answer: He quit playing because the card shark gave him a—"FISHY" FEELING

170. **Jumbles:** DIVIDE OPIATE BEMOAN TIPTOE AFRAID HERMIT
Answer: The soldier took extra target practice because he—"AIMED" TO IMPROVE

171. **Jumbles:** INDICT ARCADE NUANCE NOBODY SAILOR QUARTZ
Answer: She refused to be a wardrobe model because she—COULDN'T "STAND" IT

172. **Jumbles:** ELICIT EXPOSE CLOUDY VESTRY PRIMED JURIST
Answer: The house cleaner was hired because she had a—"SPOTLESS" RECORD

173. **Jumbles:** NICETY QUARRY MYOPIC INVOKE VACANT AVOWAL
Answer: When the rooster pranced around the chicken coop, it was—"POULTRY" IN MOTION

174. **Jumbles:** VOLUME CRABBY BEFORE DOOMED ANYHOW PITIED
Answer: Soldiers do this all the time—"COMBAT" BOREDOM

175. **Jumbles:** PRYING OUTLET PIGPEN TIMING EXTANT VENDOR
Answer: What the judges considered the winning skater's spins—THE "TURNING" POINT

176. **Jumbles:** GOVERN ENGINE TAMPER ENCAMP SHERRY INBORN
Answer: What Dad experienced when Junior unexpectedly waxed the car—A "SHINING" MOMENT

177. **Jumbles:** DIGEST MUFFIN UNTRUE GRASSY SHANTY BESTOW
Answer: What the teacher discovered when she returned from her honeymoon—SHE WASN'T "MISSED"

178. **Jumbles:** BISECT EXCITE DEPUTY SIPHON FAIRLY WAYLAY
Answer: The M.D. visited his accountant because it was time for—"FISCAL" THERAPY

179. **Jumbles:** TARGET OUTING STUDIO COMEDY DEFAME TURTLE
Answer: What the shepherd wanted to avoid when he took his flock to market—GETTING "FLEECED"

180. **Jumbles:** CORNEA ORIOLE JOVIAL TURBAN MAGNET CAUCUS
Answer: Where the owner of the seedy bar kept his money—IN A "JOINT" ACCOUNT

Need More Jumbles®?